Rudolf Laban
An Introduction to his Work & Influence

Rudolf Laban:

An Introduction to his Work & Influence

John Hodgson
&
Valerie Preston-Dunlop

Northcote House

British Library Cataloguing in Publication Data
Hodgson, John
   Rudolf Laban: an introduction to his work & influence
   1. Dancing. Laban, Rudolf
   I. Title.   II. Preston-Dunlop, Valerie
   792.8092

ISBN 0-7463-0584-2

First published in 1990 by Northcote House Publishers Ltd,
Plymbridge House, Estover Road, Plymouth PL6 7PZ, UK. Tel:
Plymouth (0752) 705251. Telex: 45635. Fax: (0752) 777603.

Typeset by Kestrel Data, Exeter
Printed in Great Britain by BPCC Wheatons Ltd, Exeter

Contents

Preface

Laban is arguably the most influential figure in dance in the 20th century, and his theory and principles of movement are as pertinent and central to man's understanding of himself in the 21st century as ever before. Laban is such a multifaceted character, with work and influence in so many different fields, that it needs time to come to terms with his life and appreciate the significance of his contribution.

It may seem strange to be introducing the work of Rudolf Laban at this point in time. Shortly after he died in 1958 more people than today would have claimed to have known about him and his influence for at that time there were a great many individuals who were applying his discoveries in several spheres of activity. But the passage of time does a number of things: it allows us to forget, it allows us to confuse, and it provides us with opportunities to set up false perspectives. Fortunately it also allows us to stand back, re-examine, and reappraise.

What, then, is the best way to introduce Laban so as to encourage an interest, an objectivity and a growing understanding of his work; how can the fundamental nature of his discoveries and the unity of his vision best be indicated? Laban's own writing tended to be on different aspects of his work only so far as expediency called for it. He began methodically enough with the idea of two basic works—the 'World of the Dancer' and the 'Script of the Dancer' —but life rarely evolves neatly and he never had the opportunity to present in written form a holistic overview.

Now, at some remove from his life and work, it is possible to look more objectively at the broad span and the central issues within it. So rather than collect together specialist contributors from each of the different fields of influence, the object has been to draw together a composite view based on over 20 years of detailed study from the authors' different professional bases.

Because this book is an introduction to Laban's work and influence, attention is focused principally on events in his life, so emphasising Laban himself and his own activities. It does not set out, therefore, to cover in any detail the independent developments in other countries, nor the developments which have taken place since his death. Where post-1958 information is included, it aims simply to give perspective.

The approach is two-fold:

Part One is a series of essays, each focusing upon a single aspect of Laban's influence while at the same time indicating the concurrent and cross-referencing nature of his life's quest. Each of these introduces his initial interest, his continuing development and gives some indication of the further progression pursued by his associates and later followers.

Part Two is a reference file, compiled by Dr Preston-Dunlop, that makes readily accessible many of the fundamental facts of Laban's work and influence. Until now detailed factual information had been hard to correlate since much material was destroyed in the two world wars. In addition, Laban's co-workers came from many different countries and languages and, because of Nazi harassment, were dispersed. Now, for the first time, this reference file chronicles events, dance works, people and writings. These references support present understanding and form a sound basis for future research and development.

Among his many talents Laban was a graphic artist and twelve of his original graphic works have been selected to show this side of his artistry. Laban's main graphic period was from 1900 in Paris, Nice and Vienna through to 1913 in Munich when he decided to devote his time to dance. He did, however, continue throughout his life to use this talent, in stage design and costume, in caricatures of his surroundings and his friends, and in painting for his own and other people's pleasure.

Together, the essays and supporting data aim to set Laban's work in context and give a thought-provoking introduction which can lead to a genuine understanding and perspective for application of his ideas in dancing and every other art of moving and being today.

Even though Laban's work is still inadequately understood, its pervasive influence is evident, and can be seen in many forms, carried out in many personal styles and diffused into many cultures and countries.

Though the Laban Centre in London is his most direct practical and academic successor, his students, both first- and second-generation, continue to establish and develop his work throughout the world. This book is another step towards meeting the desire for a greater availability of information, and a better understanding and awareness of Laban's profound contribution.

John Hodgson
Valerie Preston-Dunlop

Acknowledgements

The major resources for this book are the two collections which the authors have built up over many years. John Hodgson's personal archive and the Laban Collection of the Laban Centre have been made from interviews and donations from too many individuals to thank by name. Many of them appear in the text as involved in Laban's life and influence.

John Hodgson gratefully acknowledges the support of Bretton Hall over many years. The Calouste Gulbenkian Foundation has generously supported the Laban Centre's commitment to research and Dr Preston-Dunlop warmly appreciates the Centre's contribution to her work.

The authors are indebted to the invaluable and voluntary assistance of John Dunlop, who has undertaken the meticulous preparation of their manuscripts for publication.

Part One
Laban's Work and Influence

1 Laban, the man

Photographs of Rudolf Laban, taken throughout the 78 years of his life, reveal a man of astonishing variety. It is sometimes difficult to appreciate that all these facets were one and the same person. Laban was a complex and varied personality.

Like most of us, many of the clues to his character lie in his childhood and upbringing. The eldest child of a military governor in the Austro-Hungarian army, he enjoyed rank, privilege, travel, solitariness, considerable parental expectation and a wide variety of experiences from a very early age.

More often than not his father was absent on military duties, and even when Rudolf visited him in those far-away countries he saw little of his father since he lived the full life of any foreign diplomat in occupied territory. His mother, whom he knew rather better, was younger than her husband but she too was often away from home as the dutiful wife. On such occasions the young boy was looked after by servants or an English governess and never, in the domestic sense, learnt to look after himself. Domesticity bored him for there were always better things to do. Like many young people left often to their own devices, he learnt how to observe and how to fantasise. At home he came to enjoy myth and legend listening to his grandmother read and tell him stories. His imagination, and opportunities to participate in the local theatre, led him to re-express several of these stories in puppet plays.

He found school an unkind and uncomfortable place, far too desk-bound and restrictive to his natural inclinations, and by the time he was sent to secondary school he could only express himself in rebellion and general unruly behaviour. There was even a time when no school could or would contain him. This is not altogether surprising when one considers that Laban in his teens had already been on long journeys across strange land-masses and rough seas, taken part in vast military manoeuvres and seen sights and experienced adventure that few other boys of his age had even read about.

One side of him, then, was being educated richly, but the lack of traditional schooling left him without intellectual challenge and mental discipline, and hence without much linear logic or academic rigour. He remained throughout his life a highly creative, imaginative and lateral thinker, but not one who could easily sort out his ideas in words on the page. Though he spoke and understood several languages, he never really mastered any.

It was in the visual realm that he received most of his training. At around the age of 16 he was apprenticed to a local artist and through him developed his painting, drawing and observational skills. Here his interest in geometric shape was first awakened through being introduced to the Golden Mean and other elements of artistic law.

By the time he was fully of age he knew in his heart of hearts that it was not the military nor the diplomatic service that must claim his life. He was from Bohemia, and in the colloquial sense he was to remain Bohemian in temperament throughout his life. He was fond of dressing in unconventional clothes, wore a beard, a moustache, or was clean-shaven as his outlook or the times changed. It was quite impossible for his father—selected by the Emperor, schooled to a military outlook—even to contemplate, let alone consent to, his only son living the sort of life which he and his tradition could only believe was the life of a ne'er-do-well. So, when the artist in young Laban finally parted ways with an angry and disappointed father, it was with the secret determination that he would one day prove himself to be someone of stature, authority and credibility.

Laban remained ambitious, not simply for himself but for all that he and those who worked with him stood for. In the early days in Bratislava he had often gone alone over the Danube and, in the open air and countryside, discovered for himself the expressive pleasure of dancing and moving freely. Then, when eventually he came to realise that this was the area in which he would devote his energies, he worked not only to put himself at the top of the dance profession, but also to ensure that dancers of all kinds were seen and treated as respected artists engaged in a respected art form.

On the one hand, this meant gaining the interest of the influential. Around the Ascona period he became a Freemason, a move which clearly carried with it a number of benefits. He was interested in Masonic rituals, and in turn advised them on further uses of movement drawn from his own understanding. He rapidly rose from the ranks to higher office and influenced one of the Lodges into setting up a section for women. The Masons were also able to help him financially, but the end result seems to have been the accruing of considerable debts and a certain disillusionment all round.

On the other hand, and more fundamentally, his ambition meant devoting his energies to working out a philosophy of dance which would establish for it not simply a place amongst the sister arts but a position in the whole meaning of the universe and man's existence within it. He realised too that a philosophy would not be enough, for people tend not to accept an art form which is not in some way tangible. Painting can be handled, music has several ways of being written down, literature has words on the page, but dance at that time remained ephemeral. So a further task he set himself was to evolve a means by which dance—and all human movement—could be notated.

For most people, these demands would be enough for a couple of lifetimes, but not so for Laban. A life devoted to the study of movement was a life of change, almost restlessness. While he enjoyed working alone, he found more often than not that it was other people who brought the best out of him, just as he could bring the best out of others. Throughout his life he worked with other people: in Ascona and Zurich it was Suzanne Perrottet and Mary Wigman especially. Then he found Dussia Bereska of invaluable service, along with Kurt Jooss, Albrecht Knust and Gertrud Snell. In England he showed great shrewdness and perception in handing on specialist areas of his work to people like Geraldine Stephenson, Warren Lamb, Marion North and Lisa Ullmann. He seemed to enjoy the initial stages of thinking and theorising, and then was ready to pass on to others the more detailed investigation. He was so full of ideas that in any case it would have been impossible for him to have followed them all through.

He delighted in making acquaintances. He enjoyed the company of all sorts of men and women. He was a man of great charm and charisma. He understood others both by watching them move and by an intuitive awareness or sixth sense. In this way he found the appropriate people to undertake those areas of his research which he did not have the time or the current inclination to pursue.

He had such ability to win people that some believed he had a sort of mystique or magic. He certainly wooed and loved many of the women he worked with, though he was never very happy with just one at a time and could not settle to anything approaching domestic stability. He fathered many children, both legitimate and illegitimate, but never spent much time with any of them as a parent. He thought more of his family of dancers and would say to them, 'You are my children'.

He lived through a remarkable period of European history, from Austro-Hungarian Empire days in the 1880s to the United Kingdom in the 1950s, encompassing two world wars on the way. He worked in the major cultural cities of Europe, Paris, Vienna, Munich, Zurich, Berlin. He accepted great times and hard times, good and bad health, fame and ignominy, universal acclaim and national denigration.

There were periods of his life in which he presented himself not as the Bohemian but as the businessman. It was not simply that he chose to look like an executive, but he also displayed a remarkable capacity for organisation. He could run a short course for dancers, devise a curriculum for an avant garde school, marshal ten thousand participants for a parade round Vienna, or draw together professional dance companies from all over Europe to a pre-Olympic Games festival.

He never learnt how to handle finances, and money remained a constant cause of anxiety for him. Apart from four years as choreographer with the Berlin State Opera, he never had a regularly-paid post. When he had money, he spent it, usually sharing it with others in a feast or festivity; when he was without, it was a famine or what the goodwill of others would afford. He never owned or seemed to care about owning property, for the most part being content with a simple room to live in and no more than basic necessities around him.

He was a strange mixture of keen social awareness and remarkable political naivety. He cared passionately for people in any socially-deprived situation and remained concerned always to improve conditions for people in any walk of life. Yet as soon as the social situation moved to the political arena he seemed to lose contact and awareness. The idealist in him seemed to prevent his appreciating the intrigue, the cunning and the downright evil which could prevail on the political level. Though he worked for and under extreme left-wing and extreme right-wing regimes, he never seemed to distinguish political ambition and power from social awareness and endeavour.

For all the pressures on him, he remained ultimately an artist, dedicated and dynamic, determined and independent. Throughout it all he maintained a wonderful sense of humour. Whilst with one eye he was looking at the world with shrewd and analytical spectacles, with the other he enjoyed distorting the image, as he did in his caricatures. His wit was sometimes so sharp in its perception as to seem almost wicked. But it was a sense of humour that helped to keep and restore his and the world's balance, an artist's perception that enabled him to keep things in proportion, and even at times to laugh at himself.

2 Laban's ideas on movement

Underlying the dozen or so areas of application of Laban's work was a belief, arising from a lifetime's study of movement, which informed, contextualised and unified. He never at any point set out this philosophy in any single or all-embracing statement, but a number of concepts pervaded his activities and gave wholeness, insight and meaning to what might otherwise seem disparate areas of influence.

Laban observed and experienced. He questioned, he thought, and he examined the nature and the causes of all he saw and went through. Even before he was old enough to believe that he could have ideas about movement at all, he had 'realised', through experience, something of its basic and fundamental nature. As quite a young boy sometimes, when left alone, he would take himself off to the mountains, and there happily leaping, stretching open-armed towards the sun, he felt in touch with infinity. 'Heaven and earth are mother and father of man, I thought, and rejoiced to be a human being,' he wrote in his autobiography. He had at the outset sensed a profound relationship between the movement of the individual and the movement of the cosmos.

Throughout the Austro-Hungarian world, festivities, fairs, '. . . peasant dances, religious processions, Court ceremonials . . . were an integral part of social existence,' he recalled a few years before he died. He saw all these as richly expressive and communicative. He also noticed people at work, '. . . women carrying bricks and wood and water uphill on their heads,' and saw that their movement '. . . was straight and natural and their gait was admirably harmonious'. Men and women showed great skill in carrying out their working movements in a definite rhythm, and took a pride in the way they carried themselves. 'It was,' he said, 'impossible to miss the great importance of movement in life'.

When he was a little older, he began to look beyond the surface of movement and to consider something of its effects. At about the age of 16 he was introduced to the ceremonies of the Dervishes, and was impressed at first by the strenuous exercise that old and young undertook at daily prayers, constantly kneeling down to touch the floor with their heads. Yet even this was nothing compared with the wild whirling of the dancers who continued turning till they foamed at the mouth and put themselves into a state of hypnotic ecstasy. He saw how, in this movement-induced state, they could drive nails and long needles into themselves without showing any sign of pain. Nor was there any wound or effect on the muscle tissue afterwards. Mountain peasants had told him before that sword dances made the body immune to battle scars, and his young mind started to cross-reference and realise that movement could have a special effect on blood flow and circulation.

Through all these experiences he began to formulate a theory of movement which he felt could be all-embracing. In the first instance he saw that movement was universal. All around is change: in growth and decay, in division and union, in vibration and oscillation, in rhythm and flow—in the sea, the heavens, the earth and under the earth, in the planets, in the tides, in the mineral and the crystal. Movement is in all living things. Even when people think they are still, movement continues within them while life remains. It is movement that enables them to discern life. Furthermore, he theorised, the quality of life is directly related to the sophistication of movement. Plants, animals and humans move, but the intention of movement, the range of movements, and the varying complications of the movements provide the clues to the overall quality of the life. In plant life motion is limited to the basic needs for light and water; animals have a greater range, being able to move more freely in response to hunger, danger, kindred and so on, while man expresses, creates and relates through a great complexity of movement patterns.

Looking at the whole range of the innate and acquired impulses of man, one is tempted to search for a common denominator . . . this denominator . . . is movement with all its spiritual implications.

Laban insisted that in the human body there is a three-fold unity: body, mind and spirit. Each of these is movement-related and interdependent and throughout there is a two-way process in operation: we feel, we think and that affects and effects body movement; we move in a certain way and that affects and effects outlook and thought. It is well-nigh impossible to walk tall and open and feel 'down', or to move in a slovenly, round-shouldered fashion and have a healthy, positive outlook.

Laban was also keen to point out the purposefulness of movement. 'Movement has always been used for two distinct aims,' he wrote in *Mastery of Movement on the Stage*, 'the attainment of tangible values in all kinds of work, and the approach to intangible values in prayer and worship'. While very often it is possible to observe similar bodily movements in each, the significance of the movements is quite different. 'Man moves,' he declared, 'in order to satisfy a need'. The need may be a simple one—to get from one position to another, to lift or move something for more or less routine purposes—but it may also be a larger need of releasing energy and relieving tension. Or it may be subtler, related to the need to express one's uniqueness. This may take the form of personal modes of body language in interpersonal behaviour or of the equally personal process of creative art-making, of writing, speaking, dancing or painting, and so on. It may occur because man seeks to develop his own skill or individual competence—at work, in sport, in overcoming the environment. Movement may, however, be motivated by a social desire to interact with others in a way designed to bring about more of a sense of community and communion. Or man's aspirations may reach to artistic and religious outlets for movement in which there is greater desire for the ideal, the beautiful, the spiritual.

Understanding movements and their functions can therefore be a means of understanding people. If they move to satisfy a need to express, then by observing and analysing movement one can discern the need, and also the aims and intentions of the movement. For movement, Laban pointed out, is both conscious and unconscious. Not only do people have habitual movement patterns which are readily recognisable, but there are also 'shadow' movements of which they are quite unaware. To the knowledgeable observer these communicate information.

'The source whence perfection and final mastery of movement must flow is the understanding of that part of the inner life of man where movement and action originate.' The body itself is the base reference point for making sense of the world. While life itself will remain a mystery, the physical presence of man is the means by which he can not only come to terms with himself but also gain greater insight into the nature of his being, and of his being in the world. It is in and through his body that each individual relates to size, to texture and to time.

Laban readily brought together several of these ideas by declaring that movement, like other ways of coming to terms with the universe, has its three Rs. The first, Laban maintained, is research, for it is through study that deeper analysis and understanding can be brought about. The second is recreation, and here Laban distinguishes three kinds. There is the sport approach strongly related to potential, achievement and competition. There is the play approach with a tendency to leave reality and through a group relationship or partnership cooperatively to play together. And then the third approach is through the performance of a created work as a means of re-creation of the human spirit in the activities of dance and dance-drama. The latter may seem to some as purposeless but indeed make an important contribution to man's wellbeing.

The third R is rehabilitation and is especially needed in life today when people have, to a great extent, lost the art of moving and lost the art of understanding its meaning and purpose. The complexities, stresses and strains of present existence lead to imbalance, disharmony and unwanted tensions. Rehabilitation is needed to restore the equilibrium. In many cases movement patterns become one-sided. Some people tend to lead lives in which their actions are all carried out with rush and speed, or are all staccato and jerky, or aggressive and confrontational. Laban's realisation was that all human beings need a balance of movement, and need to learn to use space, time and differing qualities in order to be able to redress the imbalances.

Laban maintained that harmony with the outer world and within oneself comes through the use of contrasts and opposites. The practice of such activities as gathering and scattering, travelling directly and indirectly, moving with lightness of touch and with strength, quickening and sustaining, all help to re-establish the essential balance of the individual.

Another part of this rehabilitation is achieved through the

effective use of effort through every area of our lives. Tension there will be if we are to exist at all, but it is the economical use of tension which is so important. We need to learn how and when to let go, how to relax those aspects of our being not called upon to make an effort, and how at times to release all tension in that restorative relaxation which is a sustained quietness of both body and mind and not merely a slumped physical condition.

Perhaps most important of all, Laban believed, is man's neglect of rhythm. Without a feeling for and awareness of the use and function of rhythm in the body, we cannot discover the verbally inexpressible power and potential of heightened sensitivity and realisation of harmony. 'Every harmony or disharmony has an individual characteristic as has every rhythm. To explore the world of rhythm and harmony we need to enter it fully, participating both bodily and mentally.'

It is not clear at what point in his life Laban first became aware of the links between his own thinking and that of the ancient world, but the Pythagorean philosophy as set down by Plato and others interested him greatly. This study helped him to clarify and codify much of his understanding and to identify areas for further research and development. The Greek word *choreosophie* he saw as the most satisfactory term for the knowledge or wisdom of movement, with its branches in choreography, for the study of movement writing, choreology, for the study of the grammar and syntax of the language of movement, and choreutics, for the practical study of the various forms of harmonious movement.

It was just before the First World War, in Munich and in Ascona, that he began most purposefully to formulate his ideas on movement and to contribute articles on his vision and ideas to newspapers and periodicals. His summer schools and courses helped to emphasise the need and to stimulate interest.

Fully aware that it was no easy subject to investigate, he nevertheless did explore it at every level. He realised he was taking on a complex and complicated challenge but he knew it was important to attempt to put into words what he readily acknowledged was an art beyond words. He maintained that movement is 'an art of experience' which expresses the otherwise inexpressible. 'Dance movement,' he asserted, 'goes much further than words'. It was for this reason that he spent many years struggling to find the means of writing movement, not in words, but in a notation of its own.

The successful study of movement, he maintained, could only

be achieved through the dual approach of artistic practice and constant observation. Seeing himself as artist and researcher, he insisted that his collaborators were both practitioners of dance and research assistants.

Always conscious of the vastness of his subject, he remained modest about his own achievements. In later years he was still ready to acknowledge how much further it was possible to take the study. He was optimistic that 'our time seems to stand on the threshold of a new awareness of movement' and is ready to acknowledge movement as the great integrator.

His summary of his own contribution was simply to declare that he had devoted his own life to 'a search into the nature, meaning and ramifications of movement', but the fact that he was able to transfer his skill and understanding into choreography, dancing, industry, acting, education, therapy, careers advice, body language and the training of the theatre artist, is some indication of the wholeness of his insight and the remarkable universality of his theory.

3 His concept of choreology

Laban brought so much that was new to the world of dance that he found it necessary to devise new words and establish a new terminology to cover some of the concepts he was exploring. Choreology was one such word: *chore*, pertaining to dance from the Greek root (which has many associations including 'foot' and 'song') and *-ology*, a science or department of knowledge. For Laban this dance knowledge was no ordinary branch of learning and he maintained that the word covered the 'hidden order of dance'. Because it is 'hidden', that is, not immediately obvious, it needs to be sought and Laban suggested three ways of discovering this hidden order: through experiencing the physical doing of dance, through comprehending its facts, and through crossing into the world of feelings which dancing gives. In his colourful way, Laban called them the approaches of 'the biological innocent, the scheming mechanic and the emotional dreamer'. All of these, he pointed out, are necessary and important for they inform each other.

Laban's whole life was devoted to revealing this order of dance and, as he explored, he established various branches which contribute to and aid knowledge and understanding. Even though the word choreology is linked to dance by the idea of the foot, Laban knew that the centre of dance is not the steps but the whole body and that it was important to study the body, not from the point of view of physiology, but rather instrumentally, by examining it from the point of view of its function. Legs are for locomotion, transferring the weight, turning, jumping and the like. Hands are for grasping, touching, releasing, and arms for such things as gathering and scattering. Gestures slice, cut, penetrate, indicate, and so on.

Then it was important to examine the body in action in space, and to the overall study of spatial form he gave the name 'choreutics.' In order to bring further clarity and provide a frame of reference he identified the space of the individual as special, naming it the 'kinesphere', and set about providing a kind of chart for it. Using geometric shapes to help identify patterns used in everyday movement as well as in dance, he attempted to identify what he called 'trace-forms' or common routes in space. Out of this study he developed the idea of scales, notably the A scale, the B scale, axis and equator scales and others, as idealised forms of movement progression.

These could be experienced in training in order to discover something of 'the body in space' and 'space in the body'. Laban's scales in movement bear an analogous relationship to scales in music and a developmental relationship to the *port de bras* of ballet. His scales are more oblique (less upright), more off-balance (less stable) than those of ballet, providing a complementary range of spatial form.

As scales in music can be used to explore and experience harmony, so the movement scales were especially important to the exploration of harmonic properties. Using the Platonic identification of perfect forms of solids, he was able to draw attention to relationships and chart routes which passed through points of orientation by seeing the body within the icosahedron, the cube, and so on. Vertical, lateral and sagittal symmetries, reversal and repetition are all harmonic devices identifiable in dance practice and composition. This regular harmonic organisation can be found in ballet in barre work through the *en croix* use of space, and the *en dedans* and *en dehors* of movements like *rond de jambe*. Folk dance figures are often built around lateral repetitions, 'set to the right', 'set to the left' and so on but it was Laban who helped to bring the theory into a broader and more all-embracing under-standing and to relate what he called 'space harmony' with music harmony and the principles of architecture. 'Movement is living architecture,' he wrote. The body reflects the stability of architec-ture in its vertical and horizontal skeletal structure. The three-dimensionality of arches and pillars is reflected in formal gesture. The lability of off-balance weight and leaning positions, which promote motion, weave, in Laban's spatial imagination, in and around the notional architecture of the cube and return again to reflect it in moments of stability.

Although pressed by his students to give cut-and-dried methods of using choreutics in choreography, Laban always resisted. The rich variety of ways in which different people have used it, of which William Forsythe, the Frankfurt Ballet choreographer, is a recent example, justify his reluctance.

He also made a detailed study of dynamics and rhythm in movement which he called 'eukinetics'. This area became known, after 1945, in England and America, as effort and formed the basis for analytical and experimental methods of studying the dancers' qualitative use of energy. Even as early as 1912, he had accepted that there were similarities, but also marked differences, between what we know as musical rhythm and dance, or movement rhythm. Dance steps have an affinity with countable, metric rhythm, but gestures do not. Actions of the body involve both posture and gesture arising out of rhythmic impulses, each of which has a recognisable quality. The four factors which determine the quality Laban identified as space, weight, time, and flow.

The various combinations of space, weight and time he clarified as having eight peaks in all, and gave each a name related to its main characteristics, for example: dabbing (direct, sudden, light), slashing (sudden, firm, flexible), gliding (sustained, light, direct). These clearly had a relationship to the origins of classical ballet's terms *frappé, jeté, battu*, etc, but Laban was again extending the concept by seeing these qualities as only peaks in an ongoing flux of human dynamics and relating them to a central and universal theory.

These effort qualities are to some extent also analogous to colour theory, with its hue, tone, intensity and so on, a topic much discussed by Laban's fellow theorist in Munich, the abstract expressionist painter Wassily Kandinsky. Arising as they do from the impulses of the dancer, these qualities not only provide the additional colour or hue of the shape of the dancers, but they also initiate steps and shapes, and only take full form when accompanied by what Laban called the 'inner attitude'. In the 1940s he devised an effort graph symbol system for writing down complex dynamic changes so making it possible to record areas of the hidden order where mere words are inadequate.

The fourth element of the movement syntax Laban gives as relationship—between body parts, people, and the body and its spatial environment. Two strands emerge in this work, awareness and sensitivity of group 'feeling', and the abundance of group 'forms' which occur through interrelationships.

Ever since his days in Paris at the turn of the century when he first studied Feuillet's *Choreographie*, Laban had been determined to find an adequate notation for dance and movement. He knew that if dance were really to be taken seriously, it would have to be studied and analysed, for which purposes a system for making a written record would be necessary. He was pleased to study the approaches of earlier systems and move on. Almost all previous attempts at notation had concentrated on steps and positions; Laban saw that he must define the 'movement process', so achieving a graphic description of the ongoing 'flow of motion from one limb to another' which is, after all, how movement proceeds in time.

Feuillet's approach had been through floor plans presented horizontally, with the individual body seen as the vertical, additional element. Laban gave emphasis to the individual and so stressed the vertical, clearly recognising that the floor plan is the outcome of the individual's movement in space and time.

In devising a staff, he followed at first the pattern of music notation, moving from left to right across the page but, realising that the path of the dancer and the body's bilateral dimension is best seen in a vertical staff, devised his notation to read from the bottom to the top of the page. By 1928 he had established an excellent basis for its use and development in many walks of life, in many forms of dance and in many styles of moving. There was no longer a need for the well-trained reader to be familiar with the steps of a piece nor the conventions of the period.

Many of his students and fellow workers contributed to the final product, most notably Albrecht Knust, who devoted himself to it almost entirely during the dark days of the Second World War. Kurt Jooss, Sigurd Leeder and Dussia Bereska were also important contributors to the steady evolution of what was first seen under the general name of *tanzschrift*. His system became distinguished

as 'Kinetography Laban' and then took on the name given it in
the USA—Labanotation.

Amongst those developing the system in post-war years, Ann
Hutchinson's work has been especially important in promoting the
notation in the USA. Maria Szentpal in Hungary refined the
orthography of fine stylistic details in folk dance and Valerie
Preston-Dunlop in the UK developed Motif Writing in which the
choreographic intention is written down rather than the resulting
form.

The vast use of Labanotation today is impressive, from the
recording of major ballets through modern dance works to Broad-
way musicals and folk dances. For the first time dancers have a
sure means of copyrighting their choreography (an interesting
irony since choreography, of course, means 'dance writing' but, in
the absence of an adequate system until now, the word has become
associated with the act of creation).

Laban founded his first Choreographisches Institut in 1926 in
Würzburg which then moved to Berlin. This was a specialist school
and research centre for advanced work, in which choreology and
dance writing were the main subjects. Bereska was his assistant for
eukinetics, Gertrud Loezer for choreutics and Gertrud Snell for
kinetography.

Aurel von Milloss, one of the students and later a much-revered
ballet master, said, 'Laban's choreological ideas transformed the
ballet vocabulary for me. I saw for the first time its structure. His
choreology showed me how to take the steps apart and make new
movement'.

In Hamburg in 1930 Knust opened the first Notation Centre
and Ann Hutchinson founded the New York Dance Notation
Bureau in 1940. There is an International Council of Kinetography
Laban which monitors developments in the notation system.

As well as Labanotation, parts of choreology are widely used as
'Effort/Shape' in the USA, some of the leading centres being
Ohio State University, Seattle University, Hawaii University, the
Juilliard School, and the Laban/Bartenieff Institute of Movement
Studies, both in New York and in York University, Toronto.
Dance departments as far afield as Hong Kong, Adelaide, Paris,
Budapest, Jersey and London are also actively using and develop-
ing Laban's ideas. At the Laban Centre in London Choreological
Studies are offered at the undergraduate and post-graduate levels.

Because of the efforts of Laban and his followers, dance can be
studied in a way quite unknown before he undertook his profound

work on the grammar and syntax of movement, encompassing choreutics, eukinetics, instrumental body use, relationships and their notation systems. Using structuralist methods with procedures unique to dance, choreology offers a unified approach to the study of dance. Practice and theory need no longer be separated, for with choreological understanding the individual combines thinking and feeling with the doing of dance.

4 His innovations in the theatre

The fascination that Laban had with the theatre began early and remained with him through his life. As quite a young child he had seen the Kasperl Theater or Punch and Judy Show. Shortly afterwards he had his own puppet theatre and was developing original puppet plays. Even these childhood creations had plots of significance, being an imaginative blend of stories told him by his family and his own interpretations of the conflicts of the world around him.

In his teens he frequented the local theatre where he had privileged access to the whole building. He absorbed the atmosphere and was captivated by it. Already a perceptive young man he was not, however, impressed by everything he saw and heard there. He was quite quickly put off by the false and over-showy, by the petty and the pretentious and began to distinguish for himself between what he felt was art and what appeared to be merely artificial.

Over the next few years he saw most forms of entertainment, from sordid revue to highly acclaimed opera and ballet. It soon became clear to him that no matter how, or in what form, the theatre might manifest itself, at the centre of it all was human expression using the human instrument—the body. He recognised that it was through movement that feelings, moods and ideas were conveyed and that voice was part of the whole, simply another manifestation of movement.

In the 1920s, when his own theatre practice began in earnest, dance was still mainly a frontal art in proscenium theatre form. The vocabulary of steps and movement qualities was strict and, apart from the innovations of the Diaghilev Ballet Russe, limited; the role of the ballet master was supreme. Laban challenged and changed this. By examining the expressive potential of the body he opened up a far wider range in direction, plane, sphere, rhythm, shape and quality. He liberated the dancer in a way which some found shocking but none found they could ignore. He became known in Europe as the father of modern dance and his approach became known as 'free dance', 'expressive dance' and, because at that time he was working in Germany, as the 'new German dance'.

For Laban there were only two types of human activity: doing, the movement that was obviously purposeful, and dancing, done for expression and re-creation. He thus had a thoroughly unified approach to dance whether it was cabaret, tap, Charleston or classical ballet. So for the first time there was no sense in ignoring some dance forms in order to elevate others. It was more important to attempt to understand the skills involved in each, the qualities and expressive opportunities each conveyed. His own dances, then, were of a wide variety of genres and ranged from expressing his early response to nature (*The Earth*) to interpretations of classics (*Agamemnon's Death*).

Though he had a rich sense of humour, and a keen eye for satire, he established within his philosophy the fundamental concern that dance should deal with subjects and matters which held significance. So he created dances around ancient and modern myths (*Titan* and *Night*), dances based on existing dramas (*Don Juan* and Goethe's *Faust*) and dances of personal and universal experience (*The Fool's Mirror* and *The Swinging Cathedral*).

He developed solo dances and duos, dances for small groups and for large. He could and did work within existing frameworks. He choreographed works for established operas ('Bacchanale' in Wagner's *Tannhäuser*) but also looked to new structures. The dramatic in him found expression in his many dance-dramas (*Illusions* with its clear characters, plot and dramatic climax). He was fond too of the *Reigen* in which there is 'significant mirroring of the inner development of a character and never the story of external events'. He introduced the idea of a full-length abstract work which he called the dance symphony (*The Deluded*). Narrative line and abstract pattern, comedy, tragedy, history, satire, burlesque—all appeared within his repertoire.

Never was Laban's approach a mere interpretation of the music. He was keen to insist that the dance was an art in its own right and not simply the handmaid to music. Some people at the time were incredulous when he presented movement without any sound accompaniment at all. Sometimes he did this out of basic financial stringencies, but it was also a matter of policy and philosophy. Laban used small orchestras and some of the first recorded music. He drafted rhythmic scores for collaborators to work from and wrote the music for some of his early works himself. He enjoyed making use of percussion of all kinds, played by dancers as well as musicians. He also explored the effectiveness of many other forms of sound and developed especially the association of the speech choir with the dance with great success (*Faust's Salvation*).

Besides expanding the conventions, Laban maintained that dancing was for all and not just for those few who happened to conform to a particular build. After all, music happily accepted that not all singers must be sopranos, so why not acknowledge that dancers could be 'high', 'medium' or 'deep'? This variety would add to the interest and develop the expressive range, giving the choreographer opportunities for the exploration of harmonic or discordant relationships. Nor did Laban accept that professional dancing was the province of women only; he encouraged men to express their individuality and particular movement qualities and so the male dancer began to come into his own with some strong, exhilarating choreography (men played the central roles in works like *Don Juan* and *Men's Dance*).

Of course dancers must have skills and a well-trained body, but there were qualities, he maintained, that were more important than mere technique. Coordination, flexibility, control and, above all, rhythmic versatility were amongst his priorities. It was an all-round capacity to use and understand the expressiveness of the body that was needed for the modern dancer. Technical proficiency was unlikely to communicate more than circus skill. What he looked for in his dancers was the capacity to create and re-create and to explore ideas through improvisation.

This way of working put him ahead of his fellow choreographers for he did not care to tell his dancers or show them how or what should be done, a method only adopted by others much later. Making a dance was the coming together of a group of creative people who, trained in physical expressiveness, could stimulate each other to develop the final work of art. This left no room for 'stars' or 'leads' but gave clear commitment to the dance ensemble. It also demanded that the dancers were fully committed to medium, message and a great deal of concentrated work. It left no room for those who only saw in dance a means of self-display.

As the observing eye and ear, Laban's especial contribution was in enabling form and rhythm to emerge. On both page and stage he played with geometric and sculptural form, not just as interesting shapes but as tensions and effort qualities which could communicate discord and harmony. He explored polyrhythms of all kinds and was particularly fascinated by the effect gained when several rhythms took place at the same time within a group as well as within an individual.

Laban was always eager to maintain the individuality and spontaneity of each person he worked with, to draw something original from solo dancers. With crowd work he was expert at knowing how to bring individuals to work sensitively and expressively in dramatic and inventive groupings.

He was never happy with the traditional architectural form of theatre, which tended to force what he emphasised was a three-dimensional art into a two-dimensional setting. Laban experimented with various levels and shapes of platform and rostra and explored differing relationships between dancer and audience, from time to time letting the performers spill into the auditorium. Whenever he could he brought the audience on to three sides, so denying the picture-frame and reinstating the presentation as an ever-changing pattern of human relationships with all their plasticity and power. He shunned scenery preferring the dance in an open space to speak for itself.

Because the appropriate buildings did not exist he united theory, both acoustic and visual, with his own experience and philosophy and designed a theatre for dance. The plans were promoted and won an architectural prize, although the building was never realised.

His professional association with the theatre was as long and varied as his innovative practice. Beginning in Munich and Ascona he had experimented with themes, inspired Hans Brandenburg to draft scenarios and set Mary Wigman on her path to international fame as a dancer. By the outbreak of the First World War he had established a significant reputation and in Zurich his dances and dancers were sought after by the Dadaists. He began directing large-scale works with his own company in 1921, the year he became guest choreographer to the Mannheim national theatre.

The following year his company, the Tanzbühne Laban, made its home in part of the building of the zoological gardens in Hamburg and set off from there on tours, which continued until widespread inflation made touring too difficult. Laban then concentrated on the small chamber group (Kammertanzbühne

d with this group both in

her at the Bayreuth Wagner
r. At the same time he was
State Operas, a post he held
iproar when he summarily
a corps with whom he could
uvre round élitism and

on in Paris in 1932 his pupil,
irst prize with his ballet, *The*
:hat subjects as universal and
significant as politics and war could be effectively treated in dance.

In 1934 Laban was given the responsibility for dance for the whole of Germany. The Reichskulturkammer, in appointing him as director of their newly formed Deutsche Tanzbühne, gave him the opportunity to further his ambition for the dance and to foster his concern for the recognition of the importance of the art. He organised classes and courses for unemployed dancers and arranged showcase performances at leading theatres. He created the Berlin Dance Festivals of 1934 and 1935, in which the established dance figures Kreutzberg, Palucca and Wigman were presented alongside young out-of-work dancers. The programmes, too, indicated his breadth of vision by juxtaposing works of classical ballet with those of modern dance.

Laban's theatre work in England was mainly in movement work for actors. With Esmé Church at the Bradford Civic Theatre he explored movement and mime plays for actors, developing some of the work he had done earlier with archetypal characters in his dance-dramas. His services were sought in character, group and crowd work for Martin Browne's first production of the York Mystery Plays, and when illness prevented him from participating directly his role was taken over by his pupil, Geraldine Stephenson.

Although Laban's own choreographic work is not what we will primarily remember him for, his whole theatre practice remains challenging and influential. He established the importance of realising that dancers come in many shapes and styles, each with a wide variety of expressive movement. He proved the value of seeing each dancer as an artist, of seeing each dance as an experimental and creative process, and of seeing the art of dance itself as an open, free form of expression capable of communicating the most light-hearted to the most significant of themes.

5 Laban's fight for the status of dance

Most of Laban's life was a battle for the status of dance. It was a tough and arduous struggle and, though sometimes he felt that he was beginning to make some progress, the fight indeed was never over.

He first realised at home the very low esteem in which dance was held by those who were not involved with it. His conventional military father would not hear of his son becoming any kind of stage artist. Painting was '. . . more respectable than stagecraft because of Raphael and because it was generally preferred even by the Popes,' Laban recalled in his autobiography.

Then when he arrived in Paris at the turn of the century, he saw for himself something of the more public image of dancers where there were in 'low-class cabarets . . . poor devils who called themselves artists', and witnessed what some had to do in order to earn a living. Those two influences, the private and the public, drove him on against all opposition. On the one hand was the need to show, especially his father, that he was part of a noble, aspiring profession, and on the other a more universal desire to see his fellow dancers acknowledged as honourable artists.

Much of what he did practically, in the post-First World War days, contributed to challenging some and inspiring others to a better realisation of the nature of dance. His work in Munich, Ascona and Zurich caught the attention of established writers on the dance. Hans Brandenburg especially recognised what Laban was doing for and with the dancers. He saw clearly that a fresh concept was in operation, no longer with superficial entertainment at the core but with genuine and significant themes brought to life. Those taking part, too, were a challenge to former expectations. The women were not loose-living dancers, but artists of integrity and worth. Laban's male dancers were not effeminate and weak, merely supporting their female partners, but men dancing with strength and purpose, confirming masculinity and able to take a central role in the dance works.

In 1920 he published *The World of the Dancer*. For many years

Laban had been jotting down his thoughts and reflections in note form. Now he was ready to draw together these ideas and present them in a manner appropriate to his own thought process and to the subject on which he was writing. Here, for the first time, was a dancer setting out '. . . to speak about a world where language alone is not good enough'. Aware, however, that dance would never be properly accredited nor understood until someone could '. . . conquer for the dance the field of literal and linguistic expression', he skilfully sought to relate the form of the book to its content, giving himself the goal not of writing a handbook but of setting down 'thought rounds' in order to 'awaken insight into the dance'. His aim was large because he saw dance against a background of man in the universe and wrote that dance had '. . . something which fulfils the whole physical, emotional and intellectual existence'. This book made an immediate impact and Laban found himself in a position of increased respect and authority.

Such an achievement was, however, only the beginning. He knew it was also important that the dancers themselves had means of improving their professional conditions. Up to that point dancers had been of little significance—they had no means of coordinating negotiations for wages, no rights of employment nor set conditions of service and no means of security. There was high unemployment, and it was not uncommon to see dancers busking at street corners as their only means of livelihood. Laban saw that one way to begin to rectify this state of affairs was to gather together as many dancers as possible and form some sort of trade union which might one day prove as strong as that of the musicians.

It was a sound enough theory but in practice it proved more difficult to implement. Dance included a wide range of performers, and within the dance ranks there remained two camps who continued to regard each other with deep suspicion, the established classical ballet personnel and the emerging groups of modern dancers. In addition there was hostility between the professional and the amateur, between the dance artist (Tanzkunstler) and the lay dancer (Laientänzer).

In 1927 Laban, with Schlee, initiated the First Dancers' Congress, to which dancers of all groups (classical, modern, social, folk, variety) were invited. They had set up an impressive and widely-representative committee which included Anna Pavlova and Oscar Schlemmer.

Laban tended, perhaps not unnaturally, to dominate the scene— he was the general organiser, premiered three of his own dance works and was also one of the main speakers. A wide spectrum of dancers was present and there was enough good press and sufficient enthusiasm to give rise to the planning of a second congress for a year later. In 1928 at Essen, Kurt Jooss became the organiser and again there was a good attendance from all sides. Unhappily, Mary Wigman did not share Laban's vision of a unified profession and two unions resulted, one around Laban representing elements of classical/modern/social/variety, and another around Wigman solely concerned with modern theatre dancers. By the end of the year, however, Wigman and Laban were together again in public.

It was at the 1928 Congress that Laban made one of his most significant public gestures in the struggle for the status of dance. For a long time he had believed that status would never be accorded to the art until it could become, at least in part, a tangible art, in this respect on a par with music and the written word. Since he was concerned not just with dance but with the wider field of movement, he tried, tested and finally, with the help of his close pupils and associates, arrived at a notation system that could record any pattern of human movement. This was received with acclaim at the 1928 Congress and attracted the interest of several influential circles.

Laban continued to publish his ideas on all and any aspects of the dance from commenting on the Charleston as a new dance step, to commemorating the death of Anna Pavlova as part of the great classical tradition. He published in *Die Tat*, wrote for the extreme left political journals (*Der Junge Mensch* and *Die Fahne*) as well as for magazines on the right (*Die Schönheit*). He wrote articles for the professional magazines *Singchor und Tanz* and *Die Musik*, and began the journal *Schrifttanz* in 1928 with Alfred Schlee of Universal-Edition.

As all the written material by and about him helped to establish him as the 'spiritual leader of the new dance', Laban felt he should ensure that he still had a practical involvement in the dance and that it would be seen to be prestigious, sound, respected and, besides paying himself an honour, serving the ultimate cause of establishing dance as an art of significance. He accepted the post of choreographer at the 1930 and 1931 Bayreuth Festivals. This was certainly the first time in German dance history that a man of such a literate reputation had become a practicing choreographer. There in 1930 he worked alongside Siegfried Wagner and Toscanini, commanding their respect and admiration.

He became choreographer to the Berlin State Operas and when

the Nazis came to power almost compromised himself in the desire to see dance firmly established. He accepted the post of Director of Dance under Goebbels and persuaded the Reichskulturkammer to finance his courses and showcase productions for out-of-work young dancers. He managed to have dance included in the 1936 Olympic Games activities, though largely outside the main competition and beyond the nationalistic concept of the Games themselves.

Finally, however, under the Nazis he saw dance reduced in stature to its earlier position of 'Peoples' dance', traditional, folk and social dance and saw ballet again dominated by women. Although the experience affected him deeply, he did not give up, and even while he was in so-called disgrace and living in a kind of exile in Schloss Banz he continued to write about his vision of the future for dance in Germany.

The same opportunities for work in dance did not come his way again once Laban arrived in England. He found it difficult to recall for himself, or to recount to others, all that he had been through and apparently lost while in Germany, but he took those openings that did occur and brought some status to dance within the educational curriculum.

Laban's written output in England was of a different order too. Textbooks on educational dance, work, theatre and notation were completed and articles regularly contributed to and for *The Laban Art of Movement Guild Magazine*. In England he was not so much battling for the status of dance as for the acceptance of the art of movement overall. He wrote and made notes continually and many articles of stature have been published posthumously.

With the help of Lisa Ullmann's unstinting energy, Laban built on a changing climate in education. Through short courses for teachers in state education and others, he impressed HM Inspectors and County Organisers to such an extent that the authorities sought to find the means by which 'Central European Dance' (as it was then called) could become part of the curriculum. By the 1950s most local education authorities were encouraging the implementation of 'modern educational dance', as it became known after the publication of his book of that name in 1948.

The scheme, however, was dogged by qualified teacher shortage and, like other excellent ideas, became the rage for a while and then lost its impetus through insufficiently trained practitioners in a too rapidly growing field. There being no suitable area of administration in which to place the new subject, its survival was further made difficult by being placed under Physical Education instead of the Arts. So while on the one hand it gained status through sheer proliferation, on the other it all too easily lost ground by becoming an adjunct to a subject which is only superficially its sister. Ironically, Laban's fight throughout his period in Germany to distance himself from 'physical culture' was nearly lost in Great Britain.

Fortunately that setback was not for ever. Some pioneers continued to make progress and establish healthy roots because of their sound understanding of Laban's philosophy, theory and principles. Much of this has been supported by institutional recognition that dance, like any other subject, can be studied in higher education in its own right at both undergraduate and post-graduate levels. Dance research has been established using the traditional disciplines of aesthetics, sociology and history, but also through Laban's methods.

In 1962 the ethnochoreologists accepted Labanotation as their system of recording dance for morphological research, and in the 1980s choreological methods were accepted for doctoral research. So the struggle goes on with ground gained and ground lost but always, on review, it is possible to discern the vast distance travelled in establishing dance as something more than peripheral, more than superficial and more than ephemeral. Through his great personal dedication and commitment Laban set dance on the road towards becoming a thoroughly respectable and respected art. To maintain and gain further ground calls for equally dedicated and determined artists who do not look to themselves in the art but realise, as Laban pointed out, that 'art is self-denial', and individuals who seek further to promote its status must, in his words, 'transform themselves to the service of the art'.

6 His approach to the training of the dancer

Like so much of the rest of his thinking, Laban's thoughts about the training of the dancer did not take place in isolation. He did not even allow himself to think of training the dancer 'apart'.

In the early days Laban's attention was on his own dance

creations and his energies were directed towards seeing his dance
compositions coming to fruition through rehearsal, sometimes with
professionally-trained dancers, but mostly with people who had
had little or no opportunity to develop their skills outside the
rehearsals. Laban wrote, ' "Of course," people said to me, "you
will have to teach the people yourself " '. He accepted that in those
early days, 'I had to start from scratch'.

It was after having worked extensively on festivals in Munich
between 1910 and 1913 that Laban began to contemplate training
his dancers in a more comprehensive way. His first realisation was
that the dance artist, like so many others, needed a conducive
environment in which to develop. He wanted to give emphasis to
extending the individual, the whole person, rather than narrowly
training the body of the individual in certain skills. He felt it
important for them to 'get out of town and live a totally different
life'. But here was the first paradox. Although he planned for them
to have a life that was different he did not want it to be a life out
of touch. 'Alongside the arts, they must do a healthy job, preferably
farming, gardening . . . for the artistic work must grow out of the
community.' He found the ideal starting-place at Monte Verità,
near Ascona in southern Switzerland, and there began developing
his approach to training the dancer. Those Ascona days set a model
for later progress.

His plan grew around the integrated day. Work of the rural or
domestic kind was intermingled with dance workshops and voice
workshops. He modified the Delsarte pattern and called it 'Tanz,
Ton, Wort' (Dance, Sound, Word), emphasising that the dancer
needs to know the whole of his instrument and be ready to use it
expressively. This took the emphasis away from any single aspect
of the body and placed it on the balanced, harmonious expressiveness of the whole individual.

Evolving his theory went hand-in-hand with the training. He
was not interested simply in the development of a given set of skills
but eager to ensure that the daily class took place within an overall
understanding of the body and its make-up together with an
appreciation of the philosophy of dance.

Bodily expression, he saw from the outset, was a language and
he set himself to discover with his dancers something of the
language of and for the dance, calling it the 'choreological order'.
Any language needs both a vocabulary and a syntax and Laban
began the basic task of formulating and codifying the communicative means of dance.

Training for Laban and his dancers was not a question of identifying steps or foot positions or gestures or postures. He aimed to help all dancers know how to use their bodies so that they could find their individual means of expression and communication. This was, in his view, as valid for the professional performer as for the amateur who danced for experience.

Coming to terms with the instrument, the body, was only one side of the story. The dancer had to discover the relationship between the space and his own body. Training then became a question of exploring the space pattern, choosing how and where to move within the space to make these patterns. It was important, too, to be able to harness changes of time and rhythm and above all to discover how to find the wide range of textures and movement qualities hidden within the movement. Laban's dancers had to learn to be dexterous in the use of flow, know how to leap and turn. Men and women alike had to learn how to select those aspects of dexterity which could be most effective in the dance composition. Every individual learnt how to use the body they had been given. Be it heavy or light, tall or short, they had to know how to live in it and to use it in a full range of expression.

For many, dance technique means acquiring a finite and established pattern of skills which are regularly practised and maintained. These then become the vocabulary of the dance work. Laban's approach was almost the reverse of this for his aim was to give access to a vast and versatile vocabulary which could be brought to the creation of a dance, each individual contributing as a genuine artist within the overall shape of the given choreographic idea.

This approach does not lead to less skill in the dancer, but to a different skill and a more varied range. It is a lengthy process of discovery—a dancer will not find new movement until he knows what intimate knowledge of a movement feels like. Laban's methods therefore consisted of concentrated periods when detailed studies were repeated again and again, hand studies, studies in turns, choreutic studies, including studies of eukinetic nuance and partner subtleties. In this way kinaesthetic awareness was developed so that new movement could be found and not thrown away.

Käthe Wulff, describing the Ascona classes, said, 'It is so simple; first the instrument, the I, and then the Thou'. The community side of Laban's training of the dancer ensured that dancing together was contained in each class. Awareness of the presence of other dancers, of touch, of nearness, of the weight of others, of shared forms and rhythms, was a sensitivity developed to the highly skilful practice of group improvisation.

All this called for freedom of the body—no special shoes, no special clothing, but as near as possible to the natural. Often in the early days people were shocked by the fact that his dancers sometimes worked in the nude. Bare feet were always the order of the day. In any case as little clothing as possible enabled the dancer to be free within himself while also feeling in touch with his environment: the grass underfoot, the air on the skin, the sun on the arms.

It is clear, then, that Laban's attitude towards training stood in direct contrast to that of most other methods but, interestingly enough, was in no way in opposition to it. He did not, for instance, deny the five classical ballet positions of the feet nor the *port de bras*. With his demand upon spatial awareness, his practice was both more basic and more expansive. Laban's dancers were made aware of direction forward and backward, vertical and diagonal and other expansions into the three planes. Laban offered scales which could be seen as an expansion of the *port de bras*, more labile, more turning, twisting and off-balance. Gestures and postures were similarly expanded into free exploration and greater variety. Laban's emphasis on understanding and awareness and on the development of the artistic whole of the individual could give life to both a restricted and an extended vocabulary, for his basic principles only serve to place other techniques in a context.

On the matter of accompaniment in the dance class Laban started by relying upon the piano, the accepted instrument in classes then, and in many schools now, but rapidly explored other possibilities, especially percussion, because it gave him so much more freedom. He was usually to be found with a tambour or a gong in his hand, using voice and song as an alternative. He and his dancers were just as at home working without any sound at all. Listening to the rhythms within themselves, they had no need to rely upon an external musical accompaniment.

As a dance teacher he was more of a catalyst than an instructor, more of a coax than a coach, never a judge but always a keen critic, and a powerfully perceptive analyst, but usually combining several of these qualities with those of the inspirer.

Laban's work in training dancers continued from Ascona, with the outbreak of the First World War, to Zurich, where his dancers participated in the Cabaret Voltaire Dadaist events, even though their respective philosophies remained poles apart. In 1923 he set up his school in Hamburg and the Lola Rogge School still carries on the tradition there. Laban schools rapidly spread throughout Germany and indeed through the whole of Europe, both east and west.

From 1929 the Central Laban School was established at Essen and Kurt Jooss became director. Jooss was keen to find a technique drawing more overtly upon classical ballet vocabulary, but his clear grounding in the Laban approach and philosophy enabled him to produce his ballet, *The Green Table*. The Laban Diploma, set up to maintain standards and to offer status, was established. Regular attendance at Summer Schools to keep abreast of innovations was necessary to retain the Diploma. But in the political change after 1933 the Reichskulturkammer teachers' examinations, based on quite other criteria and including racial considerations, undermined the Diploma and Laban no longer examined.

In 1934 Jooss left Germany for England bringing with him the Laban heritage to set up the Jooss-Leeder School at Dartington Hall. After the Second World War, Sigurd Leeder continued the work at his Studio in London.

Laban himself arrived in Britain in 1938, just before the outbreak of the Second World War. Then Lisa Ullmann, who had been a pupil of Laban and a teacher for Jooss, helped Laban re-establish his training work in Manchester and set up a Laban School, the Art of Movement Studio, there in 1945. The curriculum of that school reflected that of pre-war German schools. The Laban Diploma was re-introduced, and two small dance companies, Young Dancers' Group and British Dance Theatre, were started from graduating students. In 1953 the school moved to a rural setting in Surrey, an environment closer to Laban's heart than the city.

The exigencies of Britain after the war meant that more emphasis for a time was placed upon educational dance at the newly-established Art of Movement Studio in Surrey. Then in 1972, when Marion North became its Director, two major changes took place. The first was the geographical change of the premises, now known as the Laban Centre for Movement and Dance, to New Cross, London. The second was the re-establishing of training for professional dancers. Today, contemporary dance technique, choreography and choreological studies form the core of the studio curriculum for the professional dance training. Training for leaders of amateur dance, now called community animateurs, goes on side-by-side with the dance theatre work just as it did in the 1920s.

It is difficult to indicate all Laban's influence on dance training in the USA since so much of Laban vocabulary and basic philosophy have become accepted parlance and common usage. However, it is clear that Hanya Holm, a pupil of Mary Wigman, set up a school in New York in 1930. She happily acknowledges that Laban's influence and theory remain at the base of her work, though she has appropriately developed it to suit her needs and personality. Alwin Nikolais, and through him Murray Louis, both in their own way carry on the tradition enjoying the influence they derived from Hanya Holm.

The Laban/Bartenieff Institute in New York, the Dance Departments of the Juilliard School of Performing Arts (New York), and the Ohio State University, are examples of major programmes in which aspects of Laban's training of the dancer are operative. The list of university dance departments offering Laban-based 'Effort/ Shape' modules is extensive.

7 His approach to the training of the actor

Almost the very first theoretical approach to expressive movement that Laban encountered was through a former pupil of Francois Delsarte while he was in Paris around 1902/3. In Delsarte's principles of voice and movement he found several of the ideas he was himself to develop later, especially those concerning the division of the body into head, torso and limbs and the three-fold approach to language through word, tone and gesture.

Although a few years later he began to concentrate particularly upon dance, Laban remained aware of the importance of his theoretical understanding for all theatre artists, and some individuals who later became actors worked within his classes. Just before the Second World War, however, specific individuals began to make more direct application of Laban's theory to the training of actors, and some directors became more fully aware of the value of his work in the theatre.

Just as with the dancer, Laban's concern with the actor was for the whole person and the individual as artist. It was not difficult for Laban or his followers to see other relationships between actor-training and dancer-training. Both were concerned with developing bodily expression and Laban had always been at pains to point out that, for any artist, speech was an integral part of this process. It was just as necessary for actors to be knowledgeable about the whole instrument as for dancers. His was not a books-on-heads approach to posture and gesture, nor was it possible to limit attention to simple techniques of moving about the stage. Actors, too, should discover the body in space and space in the body, and should know how to harness time, rhythm, and a range of textures in expressive use of the instrument.

'The actor on the stage shows in his rhythmic movements a great variety of efforts which are characteristic for almost all shades of human personality. The actor studies the movements of all kinds of people and what he observes are exactly those elements of bodily motion which are of vital interest to effort research,' he wrote later in life, indicating that other side of actors' training in movement, namely observation of others and understanding of how to translate that into impersonation and interpretation of character. The two-way process of mind influencing movement and movement influencing mind is a crucial awareness which the actor must acquire.

It is comparatively easy to appreciate how important Laban's theory is for the actor, once his broad statement is accepted that '. . . the visible and audible means of the performer's expression are exclusively movement'. 'Movement,' he points out, 'reveals many things. It is the result of the striving after an object deemed valuable, or of a state of mind'. The actor's objective can be seen and expressed in movement terms. Like Stanislavky, Laban pointed to both inner and outer motivation, but took his observations further, 'Its shapes and rhythms show the moving person's attitude to a particular situation'.

The actor needs to understand this visual and rhythmic language and be aware of the ways in which movement patterns are modified by changing situations and circumstances. Movement '. . . can characterise momentary mood and reaction as well as constant features of personality. Movement may be influenced by the environment of the mover'.

These were the principles that Anny Boalth brought to London before the Second World War. As early as 1929 she had been a dance student of Laban's in Hamburg, and she decided to return to England, where she had spent part of her childhood, to begin offering dance classes. Then in the early 1930s she started teaching for the British Drama League, applying Laban theory and principles for amateur actors on short and longer courses throughout the country. Once the war was over, such was the reputation that she had acquired that she was asked to undertake some movement work at the Royal Academy of Dramatic Art.

Laban's influence through Anny Boalth marks a considerable innovation in actor training. Prior to this, most drama schools included a ballet teacher on the visiting staff in much the same way as they might include a fencing or singing teacher but, through Laban's work, attention began to be paid to more fundamental principles and understanding of body and voice training.

When Laban himself started working in England in the early 1940s, he found the first demands on his gifts were within physical education and not until the Second World War was over did people begin to seek his services in more specific areas of the arts. He, too, found himself working for the British Drama League and this led to an invitation from Esmé Church to teach at her newly-founded Northern Theatre School at Bradford.

By this time Ullmann had already established the Art of Movement Studio in Manchester, just across the road from Joan Littlewood and her Theatre Workshop. It did not take Joan Littlewood long to appreciate the value of Laban's work in augmenting her own. She seems first to have come across his theory in the 1930s, but once they each realised that they were fellow theatre workers in the same city, it soon became regular practice for Littlewood's actors to take classes directly from the master himself (Jean Newlove assisting). Others who came to Laban in Manchester, for example Joan Plowright, intending to train as dancers, found the classes invaluable as a foundation for acting.

At RADA, Yat Malmgren followed Anny Boalth. He also taught movement for actors through applied Laban principles, having formerly spent some time as part of Kurt Jooss's company at Dartington Hall. Soon Malmgren was also teaching at the Central School of Speech and Drama, and afterwards at the Drama Centre. He drew the bases for his teaching from a course of training he had with Laban himself and from a manuscript that Laban and William Carpenter were working on in 1954, applying Laban effort actions and other movement principles to man's inner and outer motivations and intentions.

In *Mastery of Movement on the Stage*, published in 1950, Laban outlined some aspects of the expressive quality in movement and indicated that, just as movements of the voice can vary the meaning of the spoken word, so movement quality of the body contributes to expression and the mastery of body language. The whole vocabulary developed by Laban enables the theatre practitioner, whether actor or director, to become more aware and confident about grouping and movement motivation. 'A character, an atmosphere, a state of mind, cannot be effectively shown on the stage without movement, and its inherent expressiveness. Movements of the body, including movements of the voice-producing organs, are indispensible to presentation on the stage.'

Laban's work is basic in the use of period manners and movement, a sense of style, the wearing of costume, as well as the expression of atmosphere, mood and situation. 'Movement,' Laban emphasised, 'is the essential feeling of stagecraft.'

In the building of both physical and psychological roles, Laban's work indicates the interaction of mind and body so that, while emphasising one, the other is most surely drawn into play. He showed clearly the value of movement understanding in areas of broad farce and comedy, for here the actor needs the precision, timing and flexibility to preserve both energy and credibility. Laban's approach to general fitness is an essential starting point for the actor's development of his sense of space and timing, while his concepts of harmony and rhythm help the actor to maintain an economical balance between tension and relaxation. These essentials complement those of the great theorists from Stanislavsky to Grotowski for, based on observation, his principles give the key to intelligent understanding and application.

Brian Blessed and Bernard Hepton are amongst present-day actors who had the benefit of Laban's training personally. Scores of actors and directors who have worked with Joan Littlewood experienced her enthusiasm for Laban theory and principles, including Clive Barker, now a tutor at the University of Warwick, Murray Melvin, David Scase, and Philip Hedley, the present director of the Theatre Royal, Stratford. In a book on Theatre Workshop, Howard Goorney quotes from a letter which Laban wrote to Joan Littlewood. 'For the first time in this country I have met a group who is tackling fundamental problems of movement as affecting the individual actor and the group as a whole in such a way as to reflect the rhythm of contemporary life.'

A former pupil of Laban, Geraldine Stephenson is in constant demand for movement and dance work thoughout the professional theatre, and Malcolm Ranson, trained in Laban principles at Bretton Hall, almost seems to have a monopoly amongst leading stage and television directors as fights director and coach. At the Performance Arts Faculty at Bretton Hall, Laban's work forms the basis for the whole of the training of professional actors and community theatre practitioners as well as being utilised in projects which range from dance-drama based on the Greeks through Commedia dell'Arte to productions of present-day play texts.

8 Laban and community dance

There was never a point in his whole life when Laban did not associate dance with the community. Whether it was dance to be performed professionally to an audience, or dance involving lay people carried out largely for the delight and experience of the participants, it was, in Laban's view, a community act.

Even when he was in secondary school in Budapest he had formed a group of male dancers who rehearsed and performed ritual and traditional dances. When he undertook his year of military training in 1899–1900 near Vienna the only event which made it tolerable for him was the final celebration planned for the participants, the officials and the local dignatories. Laban had been asked to organise the 'artistic part' of this cadet festival, so he chose to coordinate a dance event which would bring together men from the many nations in the Austro-Hungarian Army, in costume, in national dances. In no uncertain terms he had established for himself several aspects of his concept of community dance.

But he did not dream this concept up alone. Bratislava and Vienna, where he was brought up, simply abounded with community dance. In fact, dance was *the* community expression. While he was growing up he had seen dances at weddings, at christenings, at funerals and 'within a year we sometimes danced on as many as a hundred or more occasions'.

Laban recognised in people both a need and a devotion to dance, a realisation which led him to emphasise the two-fold nature of the ideas of community dance. On the one hand, dance is an expression which arises out of the community, out of work release or desire for celebration or commemoration. There is a community of feeling which wants to, needs to, mark an occasion. On the other hand dance itself *is* community, in the preparation, in the organisation and above all, in the experience of dancing for the delight in the shared experience.

In 1912 he mounted a poster campaign for the reform of social dance and experimented in Munich through the Karneval festivities and then, in 1922, published an article in *Die Tat* in which he wrote of the festival culture as the 'dawning of a new flowering of mankind', overcoming the 'loneliness and desperation' of individuals and replacing their 'nausea caused by the social façade and religious hypocrisy'.

Due to Laban's efforts, the idea of social dance took on a completely new lease of life in Germany, and indeed wherever he taught, with a fresh sense of purpose and philosophy. His concept came as a strong challenge to the existing practice where, in areas like ball-room dancing, much of the community spirit and sense had disintegrated. In urban society especially, the festive and folk cultures had begun to disappear, with damaging effect upon the quality of human life and wellbeing.

After his summer 'Dance-Farms' in Ascona and Zurich (1913–1917), he continued to pioneer short courses and evening programmes in general contrast to the Physical Culture movement led by Bode, Loheland, Medau and Mensendieck. For Laban, exercise alone was not enough; it was the creative, artistic aspect of man's being with which he concerned himself. It was this creative use of movement that touched the deeper levels of human feeling and through an exploration of the symbolic and the ritualistic, the mythological and the archetypal, that a sense of community and individual development could take place.

Following the example of the singing choir, Laban prompted the idea of the 'movement choir'. Just as amateur singers could perform choric works within their capacity, alongside professional soloists, so the movement choir amateur dancers could work with dance soloists. Laban used the word *reigen* to mark sections of a number of 'expressive episodes' or 'movements' in a larger work. Later, when he was in England, he used the word *saltata* (as against cantata) and *saltarium* to denote the place where the dance took place.

In this format, both amateurs and professionals could experience the fulfilment and exhilaration of taking part in large-scale works, supporting each other without compromising their individuality and talent. Sometimes, too, amateur dance groups worked in the theatre. The Kammertanzbühne worked with the Halle movement choir in Laban's version of *Don Juan*. Sylvia Bodmer's and Lotte Müller's choir regularly worked in the opera in Frankfurt.

There were several other advantages to the scheme for groups could rehearse apart and come together, rather as some singing choral groups do, at the final rehearsal and the performance. This meant, of course, that the leaders at least had to be dance literate and be able to work from notation scores provided centrally. In movement choir work especially Laban's notation came into its own. The choric dance work entered the repertory of dance companies throughout Germany. Laban himself created several large-scale productions for all kinds of purposes and occasions (*Lichtwende* in 1923 and *Titan* in 1927). He worked with student assistants who went on to found new choirs and choric dances. Notable amongst his colleagues who became principal choir leaders were Martin Gleisner and Albrecht Knust. Other well-known leaders were Käthe Wulff in Basel and Herta Feist in Berlin.

By the time Laban came to publish *Ein Leben für den Tanz* in 1935, he had clearly established his ideas of and devotion to laientanz, dance for non-professionals. There are constant references throughout the book to festivals and dance creations devised for such occasions. The movement choir gave a real opening for creative large-scale dance works and an opportunity for major organisations and cities to commission them (the Vienna Pageant and the Mannheim Theatre Celebration).

Amongst the first of these choric works was Laban's creation of *Faust's Salvation* (*Fausts Erlösung*) for Hamburg in 1923. It was ambitious in both size and concept for not only was there a movement choir but also a speech choir who spoke Goethe's text. The Tanzbühne Laban dancers provided the chorus leaders and the soloists. The event was a great success and movement choirs began to be formed elsewhere in Germany, Switzerland and Austria. There were twelve such choirs in existence by 1926.

Any subject or idea was as appropriate for the movement choir as for the dance or dance-drama. Laban sometimes chose the occasion itself to celebrate with such pieces as *Dawn, Solstice,* and *Midsummer* or *Song to the Sun* at Ascona or *Everyday and Festival* at the Sports Stadium in Mannheim. Others, like Martin Gleisner, with a strong socialist commitment, gave their creations a political element. Gleisner formed choirs for young workers and in his *Red Song* he worked with Bruno Schönlanke, the radical poet, in developing a work which expressed the longings and frustrations of urban workers.

Yet on one notable occasion, Laban's work was not political enough, or at least not accommodating enough to the ideals of his political masters. His *The Warm Wind and the New Joy* was created for the 1936 Dance Festival associated with the Olympic Games, to be presented as the prestigious opening production of the new Dietrich Eckart Open Air Theatre which stood at the corner of the main Stadium. All over Germany choirs rehearsed from notation and finally brought their sections together in a grand preview in June.

Dr Goebbels, the Reichsminister for Propaganda, responsible for the Arts, was present. From that moment on Laban was in disgrace with the authorities and relieved of his post as Director of the German Dance. The piece gave too much emphasis to the freedom of the individual and not enough to promoting the Nazi party line of physical culture and folk dance for the state. Laban was devastated, and his life's work for dance seemed to be in ruins. Certainly no-one was allowed to use his name or his notation or openly acknowledge his theories.

In England, however, after the war the community dance concepts of Laban began again with the help of Lisa Ullmann, Sylvia Bodmer and Diana Jordan. Laban's recreational dance work established a foothold once more. The Laban Guild began in 1945 and, sometimes with Laban, sometimes without him, sponsored a number of dance days, weekends, short and long courses where community dance, Laban-style, could be explored. The Manchester Dance Circle began, the West Riding Choreos group was formed and in many other areas, university and college based groups came into being.

The peak of the movement choir work in Britain was the early 1960s. Two factors weakened it. The first was the shortage of good choric dances, recorded and available for group leaders to produce with their own choirs. The second was the arrival of American Contemporary Dance, bringing with it the vogue for the technique class which large numbers of young people found attractive.

The idea of community dance is growing again. Laban set out to counteract the adverse effects of the Industrial Revolution. Now with the microchip and the computer revolution there is time and a need for the revival of Laban's ideas on dance in the community. Some United Kingdom local authorities see the value of dance and the appointment of a dance 'animateur' is becoming established. All over the desire for festival is plainly evident. There is still a great European dance tradition to draw upon and, with a revival and a sharing of Laban's cultural vision, it is possible that once more dance could be the great source of community renewal and individual creative fulfilment.

9 His vision of education

Laban, like a number of other artists (Stanislavsky and Brecht for example), was an individual with an almost intuitive feeling for education. He was never in any narrow sense an education specialist, but perhaps because he saw education in the total context—as the process whereby the qualities of people are developed, taking into account social and cultural environment, rather than as a separate activity taking place in a school—he can be seen in a very practical way as a genuine educational pioneer.

Here, as elsewhere in his work, his theory was based upon experience. Formal education for him had been an unpleasant and unproductive time. His secondary schooling was as a boarder in Budapest while his parents were on military duties in Hercegovina and came as a difficult contrast to the life of adventure and activity Laban enjoyed while with his parents in the holidays. Frustration seemed to be the major outcome of institutional education and he began to realise even at that early age that expression and creation needed to be central for growing young individuals.

By the time he came to Munich at the beginning of the second decade of the century, he was concerned with the importance of learning by doing, and of the appropriate atmosphere and environment. At Monte Verità near Ascona he discovered both a conducive place and a number of pioneers whose social and educational outlook must have struck a chord of unity with his own. Otto Gross, D. H. Lawrence, Henri Oedenkoven and Oskar Graf were amongst those who brought ideas to the Mountain of Truth at the same period that Laban was there. Laban must have enjoyed exchanging views with others of like mind, which no doubt helped him clarify his own.

But practice informed Laban even more than theory and he tried out during that first Summer Course in 1913 a number of his concepts including that of regarding life itself as educational. He structured activities for his students to cross-reference, inform and balance each other. Education, he believed, was for all and at all stages of life and he appropriately began his own experiments with adults.

Both immediately before and during the Ascona period he had worked with students of Jaques Dalcroze whose theories on the teaching of music clarified his own ideas on rhythm and body awareness. The work of Dalcroze contained some useful elements which Laban could modify and contrast, especially as he worked out the independence of movement from music. It was not until he reached Zurich, after the outbreak of the First World War, that he started to plan how these ideas might best be worked out with and for children. With Maja Lederer and Susanne Perrottet he planned the 'Labangarten' both in Zurich and Hombrechtikon. Not surprisingly the curriculum was based upon the movement arts and demonstrated his independent thinking and pioneering spirit. He was definite about the need for air and light and space as the environment most likely to nurture the joy of childhood. He was clear too that childhood did not need too much adult interference. 'It may seem a paradox to state that to establish a good upbringing for children it is necessary to arrange a thorough discipline for adults, but it is true.'

The educator, he maintained is a kind of gardener nurturing and finding the best conditions for growth and development of each individual and what is good for one is not necessarily good for another. By the time he came to examine educational theory and practice in his book *Movement and Dance for Children* in 1926, he was ready to discuss his observations on child development in some detail, recognising four vital stages of growth: before school, at school, during adolescence, and from growing sexual maturity to the so-called coming of age. Identifying these stages of progression, which take place on a physical, mental, emotional and spiritual level, enabled him to clarify the aims and objectives of each as well as to plan appropriate movement and dance activities for each.

In Germany, various Körperkultur (body culture) movements of the time presented a very different philosophy—body-centred and with a single, narrow aim. Laban was concerned to spread his ideas in contrast, as he challenged the traditional concept of gymnastics with its emphasis on apparatus. He urged the authorities to replace it with a more natural approach to rhythm and harmony achieved through free movement exploration and growing confidence in the use of space and space relationships. Laban's influence remained in the private sector of education though he always looked for opportunities to extend the ideas on a more universal plane.

In 1929 he and Mary Wigman, with the backing of the unions they had started, published a blueprint for a State High School for Dance. It was revolutionary in concept, including subjects like Sociology of Dance which had never been heard of before. It was accepted in principle by the authorities, but the financial crisis of the early 1930s followed by the National Socialist government made its implementation impossible.

When, during the Nazi period, he became director of dance activity Laban did not confine his attention solely to the artistic but continued to look for educational openings in his work with both professionals and lay people. But for the most part the climate was against him, and Germany remained attached to the idea of 'drill' in all aspects of education and held strongly to the doctrine of unity of the masses rather than freedom of expression for the growing individual.

In England during and after the Second World War, the atmosphere was quite different. The educational concepts of John Dewey and others had already begun to capture the imaginations of a number of leading figures in the educational field, and the war gave people a determination that a new and more ideal approach must be found. Laban, because of war conditions, was obliged to live in Wales and Lisa Ullmann found work for them both amongst the physical education advisers. After the war the shift in thinking was marked by the change of subject title. Whereas in pre-war days gymnastic activities has been referred to as 'physical training', now the authorities referred to such activities as 'physical education'.

Laban's whole concept seemed right to British educators. Here was a basic philosophy together with a new approach to the physical side of school work with a vocabulary, basic principles and a holistic view of the individual. The news spread slowly at first but once the first pioneers had shown its worth, more and more interest grew until local advisers and national inspectors of education took it on with enthusiasm.

More guidance was needed for teachers and so Laban brought out his book *Modern Educational Dance* in 1948, in which he not only suggested movement and dance themes but also argued the social, historical and personal importance of dance. Here he again set out his beliefs in wholeness, balance and harmony and talked of, amongst other arts, the 'art of movement'. The concepts in his 1926 book on children's dance were developed here through the presentation of sixteen themes, divided into work suitable for the four age groups named in the earlier publication.

That the Ministry of Education had, by 1952, espoused Laban's ideas is reflected in the publication of their handbook for Primary Schools relating to physical education, now given the title *Moving and Growing*, in which his views are clearly evident as an ingredient. HMSO also published *The Story of a School*, describing the Birmingham headteacher who transformed the whole of his junior school curriculum, building all the work around movement activities, with remarkable results both in the morale and atmosphere and in its academic progress. Laban's influence in both these endeavours is direct.

There developed a great need for adequately-trained teachers who could teach movement and dance in the schools and, first at the Art of Movement Studio in Manchester and then from its new home in Addlestone, Surrey, Ministry of Education one-year courses recruited men and women for intensive training. Laban's influence was taken keenly into every training course for primary teachers in the country and movement usually featured as a core element in secondary work especially.

At the Art of Movement Studio in Addlestone, Laban saw something of his dream of an educational environment come to fruition. Here was light, air and open country, and an opportunity to encourage students to relate movement and life, dancing and doing. Gardening, jam making, pottery, housework were all part of the normal curriculum. Classes outside on the flat lawns were commonplace.

Amongst the first Laban students to publish in the field was Joan Russell with her *Modern Dance in Education* in 1958. The 1960s particularly witnessed further application in various aspects of the school curriculum. Laban's *Modern Educational Dance* was reissued in a revised edition in 1963, the same year that Valerie Preston brought out *A Handbook for Modern Educational Dance*. Violet Bruce followed by publishing *Dance and Dance Drama in Education* and John Wiles and Alan Garrard made special application of Laban's ideas in secondary school drama with their book *Leap to Life*.

This boom continued through into the 1970s but by the middle of that decade the educational climate was changing. Financial cuts were made throughout education and the training of teachers was no longer seen as such a distinct vocation. Colleges where hitherto only teachers had been trained now began to diversify, and the focus was placed more upon a degree followed by teacher training for those who wished to work in education. Subject-centred education made Laban's vision seem out of place. Partly through this atmosphere and partly through Department of Education funds being diverted elsewhere, the Laban work in education lost many of its opportunities.

It is hard to appreciate fully just why this great vision of Laban's should have become so quickly out of fashion in Britain, although it has re-emerged in other countries, notably Canada and Australia, which the classes in the Dance and the Child International (DaCI) Festivals illustrate. In a time of escalating technology, the need for physical expression and self-realisation is ever more present. In Laban's words there is still a need for '. . . the growing youngster to be guided through these reefs to a living knowledge and a will to action'. Especially at the present time in education there is a need to rediscover something of Laban's vision of education so that tomorrow's citizens can know how to enjoy moving and how to apply its confidence and pleasure in a holistic way, throughout the rest of life.

10 His concept of work

It is extraordinary to find anyone capable, within a span of ten years, of being both choreographer to the Berlin State Opera and an adviser to boilermakers in Huddersfield. It is even more unusual to find someone who not only understands the relationship between these two occupations but also is able to discuss them as being different ends of the same spectrum.

From quite an early age Laban had seen the connection between life and leisure, work and play. Brought up in the multicultural Austro-Hungarian Empire he had observed people from many backgrounds working at one occupation during the day, and then at night using very similar patterns of movement in their dancing and relaxation. There were sowing and reaping dances, fighting and other combat dances, as well as dances that were a part of worship. It seemed that man needed both to link work with the rest of his life and to find some complement to it.

Growing up as he did towards the end of the 19th century Laban observed what the Industrial Revolution was doing to man's pride and interest in his work. He observed that the machine, with its 'clumsy imitation of animals', though it does not feed on man's body, flesh and visible form, is nevertheless capable of feeding on his soul. He also witnessed, however, the approach of craftsmen and women who enjoyed and took a pride in their work. He saw too that there was '. . . hardly a trade which in its manual operations does not have a tradition of working movements and also a festive application of them'.

As an army officer in training in Wiener Neustadt in 1899–1900, Laban first came face to face with the conflict when in the railway workshops he had to learn how to handle machines. Thrilling though at times he found some of it, he could not help noticing the awesome consequence of its misuse—the servant machine becoming the tyrant monster. Though he saw industrial advance destroying others he determined to retain a more ideal view of the man/machine/work relationship and to search for ways of achieving it.

The key towards understanding work, he realised, was to understand its rhythms and its efforts, and to harness these in such a way as to contribute to the overall balance and harmony of the individual rather than allow the occupation to destroy them. Work and play need correlating rhythms. He made one or two early unsuccessful attempts to set up communities where work and play could be related. Then when he began his Summer Schools in Ascona in 1913 he built on the Monte Verità tradition and included such items as gardening, sewing costumes, making sandals, domestic and culinary activities as part of the students' programme. When war came in 1914 he tried to continue the practice at Hombrechtikon.

Many of his ideas came together in 1929 when he was invited to Vienna to direct a pageant procession for the trades and crafts of the city. It was no easy task for Laban was eager to involve the whole of the workforce in what he saw as 'a giant snake, seven kilometres long, with about ten thousand participants, decorated floats, costumes and bands,' moving through the great Ringstrasse. In spite of the discouragement and disillusionment he felt at seeing 'the misery caused by loss of loyalty to work,' he set about the gigantic task of 're-awakening in working people a feeling for their work rhythm'. Through this enterprise he studied a great variety of trades and worked with laundry girls and milliners, metal workers and farriers, shoemakers, tailors, tanners, bakers and hundreds of other craftsmen.

By the time Laban came to England in 1938 he had already clarified his concept. It was based on the belief that 'a simple style of living' is 'one of the most important sources of human happiness'. Within this lifestyle, there needs to be healthy work and festive occasions which will build a strong personality to enable man to rise 'into those spheres which distinguish man from animal'. In this ideal, emphasis was laid on the sense of a communal culture which included work, and was also 'intimately bound up with the development of the self'.

Soon after his arrival, the country was at war. Able-bodied men were called up for National Service and those remaining on the home front were required to accomplish all the work that was left. It was important to get the most out of every worker who was urged to exert himself to the limit. In the midst of this Laban was called upon to play his part in the war effort.

In the first instance F. C. Lawrence of Manchester made contact with him to find out 'what connection notating movement might have with work study and the treatment of incentive in industry'. Lawrence's firm had been using work study approaches in their capacity as industrial consultants but felt unhappy at the simple stop-watch approach in improving efficiency. Lawrence found in Laban not just someone who shared his concern for the person doing the work but someone who could put into practice a realistic approach towards mind, body and the whole person. Instead of merely examining the operations or unit of operation and timing these in order to find an average, so as to speed up the process, Laban began to analyse each action and see what lay behind it.

Laban's total concept of life and the place of work within it enabled him to apply his understanding directly to the factory situation. If the individual's action was to be developed, then the change must begin with the individual himself. 'Few people,' he wrote in *Effort*, 'realise that their commitment in work and their happiness in life . . . is conditioned by the perfect development and use of their individual efforts.' Laban, in arguing against previous studies, maintained that '. . . what has been taken so far as the basis of examination and test was but the surface indication of effort, *not the effort itself*'. He set himself the task of penetrating to the core of man's effort.

The key to this investigation of the very nature of effort was in the awareness and practice of its rhythmic character. His life-time study of rhythm in bodily motion enabled him to '. . . compile a systematic survey of the forms effort can take in human action'.

Because effort is variable and made up of many complex rhythmic movements, the process of assessment had to be detailed and thorough. Once rightly assessed, individual effort could be changed by training.

Laban's approach was to take workers in groups away from the factory bench, through carefully planned movement sessions enable individuals to find their own rhythm and, by compensation, to adjust the whole balance of their personal way of functioning. Strong movements are compensated for by light, narrow-ranging by wide, limited movement of hands and arms by full bodily activity and so on. Balance and equilibrium are only restored by activity of a contrasting kind, not by total inactivity and slump.

But employment strategies were never a simple matter of expediency to Laban. His approach was threefold: to explore individual potential, to train, develop and extend that potential, and then to decide on placement. The situation in war-time Britain demanded that women should do the work previously undertaken by men. Laban had no problem in dealing with the need but was more interested in taking the matter further through challenging the stereotypical approach based on gender—he evaluated individual potential regardless of gender.

The Laban/Lawrence method achieved great success with a large number of firms including Dunlop Tyres, Mars Confectionery, Pilkington's Tiles and the Saw Mills at Dartington Hall. Laban's expertise was also called on by the Air Ministry to assist in devising a more effective way of parachute jumping.

There were several offshoots of Laban's industrial training and research. The idea of 'Latent Effort Capacities' has been further developed by students of Laban. Marion North pioneered a method of career counselling which set out to relate young people to jobs most conducive to personality through movement analysis. At the other end of the industrial spectrum Warren Lamb set up a consultancy for management selection, based on the belief that movement can reveal capability not only in conscious movement but also through those unconscious patterns which Laban called 'shadow moves'. The demands on a managing director, on a finance executive, or a salesman, can each be determined and the potential of an applicant to work in a team can be assessed by considering the complex information provided by an individual's use of space, pressure, time and flow.

The Berlin dancer and dance teacher had become the Manchester industrial consultant. Only to the casual observer do they seem extremes. If all life is movement and all movement has its rhythm, then the fullest way to meet and derive the most from life is to see its different aspects as change and development in the overall rhythmic patterning. One man's work is another man's recreation and the way to enjoy both is to understand the first principles of alternating satisfying work with festive occasions, both growing out of a genuine sense of community.

11 Laban's work in therapy

The rediscovery of dance as a means of education and therapeutic treatment in our time originated undoubtedly from the aesthetic pleasure experienced by some teachers, doctors and industrial welfare workers. They came to us, the modern dancers, at first sparsely, one by one, but later in increasing numbers, to ask, 'Couldn't you do this kind of thing with our children, our patients, our workmen?' So we did and with quite unexpected results. Not only did the children, patients and workmen enjoy themselves, but some of them seemed to be changed in an inexplicable manner. The head-mistress of a school in which such dancing had been arranged was surprised that a child, considered to be, 'dull and back-ward,' suddenly became, 'lively and interested even in in-tellectual studies'. This might seem like 'magic' so long as it cannot be explained and it took us a considerable time to investigate the rational background of such effects.

At the basis of all Laban's theory and principles there is keen observation together with tested intuition. It is often reported that Laban would prefer to have a meal at a railway station than in a quiet restaurant since he liked to take every possible opportunity to watch people's movement behaviour.

When he was in Ascona at the Monte Verità resort, a sick woman confined to a wheelchair had come to him for solo lessons. Laban enlisted the assistance of Mary Wigman, who protested at what she considered a dangerous escapade. Wigman was there to demonstrate and she watched too, amazed as Laban made the sick woman '. . . relax her head, move her shoulders, her arms and her

beautiful but rather dead-looking hands'. Later he got her to lift
her legs and move her feet. In Wigman's own words, 'The result
was incredible. The sad face lit up again. She dared to move and
discovered that she could move. After a while she was able to walk'.

That situation was not as outrageous as Wigman had at first
imagined. During an earlier period in Paris Laban had spent
considerable time studying the structure of the human frame, its
bone, musculature and nervous systems, as his detailed drawings
from that period (1900–1910) beautifully testify. He had also made
a study of the relationship between the disturbed mind and body
movement. He lived for a period not far from the lunatic asylum
at St Maurice where he visited and made observations of the
patients and the ways in which their disorder manifested itself in
the imbalance and disharmony of their movement patterns.

Laban's tentative and intuitive beginnings first found their
theoretic confirmation in Zurich. There, during the years of the
First World War, he encountered the analytic psychology of Carl
Gustav Jung, who had just established his own methods in contrast
to the psychoanalysis of Sigmund Freud. Jung's extroverted and
introverted personalities were evident to Laban in movement
behaviour in inward flow and outward flow, movement capacities
which were observable and trainable.

Similarly, the conscious and unconscious realms identified by
Jung, Laban observed, were manifest in movement as overt and
'shadow' moves, both postural and gestural. Shadow behaviour
was considered by Laban to be evidence of deeply-embedded preferences in the unconscious. His belief that movement was a mixture
of the motion factors of space, flow, weight, and time, directly
related to Jung's concept of the four functions of the mind:
thinking, feeling, sensation, and intuition. Observation led Laban
to the conclusion that each function was evident in one motion
factor. Thus thinking was manifest in spatial changes, feeling in
flow changes, sensation in weight, and intuition in time changes.
This apparently simplistic correlation masks highly sophisticated
observations and confirmations of how the complex use of the
functions of the mind shows in behaviour. Laban's term 'inner
attitude' was built on this period of intense work.

Laban's effort theory, then, reflects several Jungian concepts.
Laban's later clarification in the 1950s of effort behaviour, in terms
of individual preferences, developed into his theory of moods and
drives, and out of this work his personality assessment methods
began.

Laban wrote that, 'Values are attached by man to his own and other people's movement capacities. "Love, sacrifice, courage" are all values only possessed by man, not by the animal kingdom'. These values are shared collectively and create community feeling. They are expressed in movement and in ritual. When value systems go awry, when qualities like aggression, hatred, or persistent slothfulness override positive values, the movement patterns reflect the change.

It is only a short step from the understanding of fundamental principles of personality and their manifestation in movement, to the development of treatment for mental illness or, as Laban saw it, for personalities whose movement life and inner effort were out of harmony. 'Remedial measures must re-awaken lost qualities,' he said. Movement training can discharge inner states, disperse them, resolve them, and can also intensify them. These are basic beliefs underlying Laban's initial schemes for treatment through dance therapy.

Apart from the occasional therapeutic engagement, however, Laban did not develop therapeutic practice until he came to the United Kingdom but he continued to deepen his awareness and insights. In the early 1950s he met Irene Champernowne and her husband at their Withymead Centre for psychotherapy. He was able to relate his understanding to their approach to Jungian analysis, and schemes were formulated whereby Laban would have given a great deal of time and expert advice to the Centre. However, a heavy programme of work in other fields, together with his increasing ill-health, meant that the full scheme never came into operation though the plan was carried out on a smaller scale by assistants.

Laban's own work in therapy can be seen as primarily preparatory. The second generation has been able to combine his insights with established physical and mental therapies to create new treatments, some of which are now accepted by the medical and educational authorities, although some are still regarded as 'alternative'.

Several of Laban's pupils developed their understanding of his principles in the USA, notably Irmgard Bartenieff, and also Trudi Schoop and Lilian Espenak, students of Mary Wigman, who all made contributions to therapeutic practice. The independent pioneering work of Marion Chase and that of Laban form the basis for much movement and dance therapy work. In the United Kingdom several people have developed strands of Laban's therapeutic work in their own way. Especially notable is Veronica Sherborne's work with handicapped children and the work of Walli Meier in special education.

Laban never managed to complete a book on his therapy work although he was actively working on one in his last years which has not been published. He did, however, write some articles and his speeches on psychology and movement are reported. Marion North's *Personality Assessment through Movement* is the most directly Laban-based publication in the area.

The movement therapy branch of Laban's work has developed a long way from his intuitive beginnings, but is even so still in its infancy. It is now possible to gain recognition from the medical authorities in some countries through qualifying examinations such as those at Hahnemann University, Philadelphia and the Laban Centre, London.

12 Laban, fitness and health

The application of Laban's theory and principles to the world of fitness and health challenges many other approaches, not least because many of them focus almost entirely upon the physical and the physiological to the exclusion of anything else, and many more focus even more narrowly on a particular aspect, such as the building of strength, muscle, stamina and the like. Laban's holistic response to life has far-reaching implications and prevents over-emphasis in any one direction, while his overall goal of harmony and balance provides an ultimate objective for the fully fit and healthy individual.

Laban was very aware of the research literature which enumerates all the bones, muscles and nerve fibres active in body motion. He was, nevertheless, keen to point out that although all healthy bodies consist of the same skeleton and the same neuro-muscular apparatus which sets the articulation of the skeleton in motion, '. . . it does not contribute to the study of movement unless one understands the latter as a unitary function of body and mind'. He maintained that the uniqueness of each individual personality demanded a more complex approach.

Once unity and complexity are clearly understood, identifying specialist functions of the body are both possible and desirable.

Here Laban saw three areas which he distinguished instrumentally: the head, concerned with mental activity and the source of all the senses (only touch being possible elsewhere); the trunk, where all the organs of digestion, purification and so on are housed, and the limbs (legs and arms) concerned primarily with mobility and gesture.

Much old-style 'keep fit' concentrated upon the bending and stretching of the trunk and limbs in repetitive ways and in neat straight lines. Equally neat and uniform was the quality and strength of movement called for and usually the timing remained brisk and uniform. The present-day return to aerobics introduces similar limitations. Yoga, while being also concerned with the contemplative, operates only in one dynamic. Laban was concerned with the development of suppleness, stamina and strength, but he emphasised that the whole being needs more. The body on the physical plane should be flexible, dexterous and coordinated but each individual, having achieved this, needs also to be able to make good use of it and to know how to involve each element with economy for his fitness to be of any substantial use to him.

Anyone aspiring towards health must realise the nature of economy of effort and recovery. Laban pointed out that it is not always an easy matter to distinguish one from the other since what on one occasion may be 'an effort projecting power into the world' may on another occasion be seen as a recovery action served by the effort 'in order to regain lost power'.

He never missed an opportunity to point out that 'Life . . . has a rhythm' and that besides the rhythm of work, recreation and sleep, there is also the rhythm of replenishment of energy, of revitalisation of spiritual and mental resources. These were the fitness aims of Laban's recreation classes.

In this, his approach to exercise was altogether more 'playful', more experimental, explorative and therefore more creative and expressive than most others. He was not concerned simply with the elementary functioning of the body, but was eager to teach that the fitness is for something which always includes expressive and emotional involvement. To develop one without the other encourages a separation of mind and body, while health education should emphasise unity. Laban's method develops a growing confidence at work, an assurance of the person in general spatial orientation and in relations with others. A conscious awareness of forcefulness and delicacy, speediness and sustainment builds capacity to cope with work, environment, and people, and hence in fitness to live.

Laban had a point of view on food. Clearly food must be nourishing to provide the vitamins and other resources that supply the fuel but the foodstuffs themselves need a variety of qualities. Just as the outward effort needs to keep the balance by a variety of heavy, light, direct and indirect etc, so the internal organs require a balanced motion through coping with coarse and fine foodstuffs, and liquids as well as solids. Their motional as well as their chemical action is significant for health. Movement is continual within the body, from breathing, heartbeat and blood flow and the constant movement of the digestive and excretory systems. To ignore this side of being is to bring about an imbalance, and full health cannot result.

At the centre of all fitness is the need to learn the art of breathing. Most people assume that breathing comes and remains a natural part of living. They take for granted that the rate of breathing will alter and its rhythmic pattern change as the demands of the blood stream and so on change. Awareness of the rhythm and pattern of breathing, Laban wrote in his first book, is important simply because drawing in the breath of life is central to so much of our activity. Understanding the rib-cage and its points of expansion, together with some training in the more expansive use of the lower chest, can aid individual oxygen supply and control as well as its economy of use. Breathing is central to the demands of effort and recovery, for unnecessary tension created by the ineffectual use of breathing often occurs because of disharmonic inner states of mind.

Mental health and physical health cannot be separated, in Laban's view. His observations have made it clear that there is two-way interaction between mind and body. Mental health and attitude affect bodily health and attitude, and the pattern also works in reverse, bodily health and attitudes affecting mental attitudes and health. Any programme seeking full fitness and health needs therefore to take this phenomenon into account. In this light it is possible to see why Army training confines itself to the parade ground Swedish-drill approach, training the limbs and the person in straight lines. Emphasis in the physical training is on rigidity, uniformity and directness and in this way the minds and responses of its recruits are also being trained in mental attitudes of a particular kind.

Quite small changes in the teaching procedures of a recreational class have widespread repercussions. Working in a circle or all facing the front, facing a direction of your choice, choosing where to stand in the room or going where you are told—these are simple ways in which independence and assurance of self are confirmed or diminished.

Laban was associated by other people with Körperkultur, Bode, Loheland and Mensendieck, but in fact he dissociated himself from them firmly, emphasising that the expressive in movement is essential and that an artistic element is the way in which that can be offered opportunity to develop.

While in Germany in the 1920s, Laban began to write about some of his ideas in his books, *Movement and Dance* and *Children's Movement and Dance*, being careful to point out that he was not talking about the gymnastics which made '. . . use of artificial aids or means of movement as being only a variation of physical exercise'.

In England during and after the Second World War he captivated the world of women's physical education and many of the teacher training colleges introduced Basic Movement and Educational Gymnastics. Ruth Morrison's innovations in using Laban principles, both of movement and of education, transformed the 1933 syllabus of Physical Training into a creative experience attempting to educate the person to cope with the environment and challenge. Although Laban was invited to some of the men's physical education colleges, Carnegie for example, his reception there was more hostile. Men seemed too entrenched in the rituals of drill and sport to be able to adjust to Laban's new and radical philosophy.

However, the Keep Fit Association, for women's recreative movement, revolutionised their methods, changing from a traditional drilled approach to one taking on those aspects of play, exploration, and social interaction which could be acquired by their teachers in short courses.

Laban was never the best example of a person ready to follow his own ideas thoroughly himself. But throughout his life he had remarkable carriage in spite of a back injury which he sustained during a performance at the age of 50. He also maintained agility. At 70 he could still undertake an impressive aerial leap across the stage.

He was, however, dogged by poor health for most of his life. His often inadequate early financial state meant that he ate spasmodically with insufficient of the proper foods, a situation which led to illness in later life. He was greatly troubled by self-doubt and fits of deep depression, and only towards the end of his life did he begin to apply his own remedies to himself. He much preferred natural cures and so-called 'alternative' treatments to what he regarded as the one-sided approach of the medical profession.

It was his followers and associates who proved the real value and practical application of his theory. A great many of them lived to a remarkable old age, enjoying both physical and mental fitness. Suzy Perrottet moved like a girl of 18 when she was in fact 90 years old, and Maja, his second wife, managed to remain positively radiant at the same age even after a very tough and strenuous life. Sylvia Bodmer, Herta Feist, and Käthe Wulff are further examples of women who practised Laban's holistic theories of fitness and have lived active lives into their 90s.

Longevity can be gained and painful ill-health can be avoided without a great deal of movement activity. But if Laban's statement that it is possible to discern the quality of life by the quality of movement is valid, the idea of simply being a survivor or even a very one-sided human being has to be rejected. A balanced approach to health and fitness through movement can go a long way towards ensuring a far richer range and quality of life for both body and mind, and Laban has laid an important foundation.

Part Two
Laban: A Reference File

13 A short chronology of principal events and influences in Laban's life

This chronicle is a selection from a much more detailed and referenced document. It concentrates on main events initiated by Laban himself, and gives some indication, in the indented items, of the work of other people inspired by him, or the events of the times which impinged on him. Deliberately, all reference to his personal life is omitted except where it is deemed to influence his work, as for example in his marriage to Maja Lederer.

Names are written as they appear in the original documents, although English translations and spellings have been used in the essays in Part One.

1879 Born in Bratislava (also known as Pozsony and Pressburg), Hungary.

1891 Travels to the Balkans with his father.
Learns folk dances of Eastern Europe. Encounters Sufi religious dances.

1899 Military cadet at Wiener Neustadt; directs folk dance festival at final cadet celebration.

1900 Studies art briefly with Hermann Obrist in Munich.
–09 Marries Martha Fricke (painter, d. 1907).
Studies at Écoles des Beaux Arts in Paris.
Encounters Delsarte system of gesture.
Encounters Rosenkreuz philosophy.
Has painting studio in Montparnasse.

Works in Paris, Nice, and Vienna as artist, illustrator.
Experiments with movement forms, especially group
improvisation.
Commences systematic observation of behaviour.
Presents *La Fête du Tigre* in Nice informally.

1910   Marries Maja Lederer (singer).
Lives in Munich until autumn 1914.
Works as painter and illustrator.
Studies old notation systems and Noverre.
Encounters Mensendieck and Bode, Körperkultur methods,
and Dalcroze.

1912   Organises some Karnevalzeit entertainments.
Decides to focus his life on dance and movement.

July   Starts experiments in releasing dance from music.

Autumn   First formal dance work created, *Die Erde* (parts only).

1913   Has poster campaign for the reform of social dance.
Organises Karnevalzeit entertainments.

Jan.   Opens 'Atelier für Tanz und Bühnenkunst R. v. Laban-
Varalja', in Klarstr. 11, Munich.
Experiments: with new structures for music composition;
with a primitive movement notation system; on separating
dance from drama and mime.

July   Opens summer 'Schule für Kunst' at Monte Verità, Ascona,
with apprentice teacher assistants: Maja Lederer for singing,
Susanne Perrottet for music, Karl Weysel for painting. Marie
Wiegmann arrives as pupil.

Oct.   Returns to Munich. Opens 'Schule für Tanz-Ton-Wort';
Perrottet assistant; Wiegmann, Weysel, Jo Meisenbach pupils.

Autumn   Starts performing and giving lecture/demonstrations with
Perrottet and Wiegmann.

1914
Jan.–   Major season for Karnevalzeit productions.
Feb.

April   Labanschule performances with Wiegmann as
Meisterschulerin and partner Weysel.

May–   Second season at Monte Verità for 'Tanz-Ton-Wort';
July   Gertrud and Ursula Falke, Käthe Wulff, Laura Österreich,

Sophie Täuber join the group.

July   Rehearses Hans Brandenburg's *Sieg des Opfers* for Cologne
            production. Gertrud Leistikow soloist, with Wiegmann.

end
July   War declared.

Autumn   Remains at Monte Verità.
            Works with Wiegmann on space harmony, notation, and
            rhythmic harmony.

1915   Great financial and permit problems for living in Switzerland.
            Moves his wife and family to Hombrechtikon, Zurichsee,
            attempts self-sufficient economy.

March   Opens 'Schule der Bewegungskunst' at Oetenbachgasse 24,
            Zurich.

April   Lectures, with Wiegmann dancing, at 'Kaufleuten', Zurich.

May   Opens second premises at Seehofstr., Zurich, assistants
            Perrottet and Wiegmann.

Summer   Runs Hombrechtikon as a summer 'dance farm', and the
            'Labangarten' for children, Lederer assisting.

Autumn   Gives lecture series on dance history.
            Shows interest in Freemasonry.

1916
Jan.   Permission to stay in Switzerland granted. Continuing
            financial difficulties.

Feb.–   Performances by Labanschule, especially Wiegmann with
March   Clara Walther all over Switzerland.

            Dadaists open Cabaret Voltaire.

Spring   Opens third premises at Seegartenstr., Zurich.

April   Presents *Der Spielmann*, choreographing, writing music, and
            designing costumes, at Seegartenstr. and at Kaufleuten.
            Moves his wife and family to villa in Dietikon, suburb of
            Zurich.

Summer   Attends several Dada manifestations. Close ties between
            Dadaists and his dancers.

Autumn   Continues teaching, and working on choreology; Wiegmann
            main assistant, Perrottet for music and children.
            Dussia Bereska joins the group.

1917
Mar.–   Perrottet, Täuber, Walther, Wulff, and other Laban dancers
May   perform regularly at Galerie Dada.

May–   Gives several Labanschule performances.
June
             Wiegmann gives her first solo evening at Pfauentheater.

July–   Goes to Monte Verità. Initiated into the 'Vesta Mystica'
Aug.   Masonic Lodge. Opens Women's Lodge.
             Presents *Die Sang an die Sonne* at major Orientalischer
             Templar-Orden meeting.

Autumn   Returns to Zurich.
             Gives several Labanschule performances.

1918   Creates *Grimasse des Sultans*; dancers Perrottet, Wulff,
             Bereska and Labanschule students.
             Seriously ill with 'flu epidemic.
             Active Freemason.
                 Perrottet runs Labanschule.
                 Wulff continues with Dadaists' performances.
                 Weigmann 'retreats to convent'.
                 War ends.
             Preparing material for his first book, *Die Welt des Tänzers*.

1919   Illness continues, renewed 'flu. Severe financial problems.
             Drawing and painting to earn.
                 Labanschule, run by Perrottet and Wulff, gives
                 performances.
                 Dada performances continue.
             Gives exhibition of drawings in Nuremberg and 'other cities'.
             Continues preparing material for *Die Welt des Tänzers*.

Nov.   Moves to Bereska in Nuremberg. Maja Lederer separates and
             returns to Munich with young family.

1920
Spring   Moves to Stuttgart.
             Opens Labanschule at Eugenplatz 5. Bereska collaborator.

Summer   Holds Summer School at Cannstadt.

Autumn   *Die Welt des Tänzers* is published by Seifert.
             Moves Labanschule to premises provided by City of
             Stuttgart.

1921   Labanschule increases; Khadven Joos, Albrecht Knust, Edgar
             Frank, Herta Feist, Jens Keith join him, also Friedrich

Wilckens, musical director and composer.
Neue Schaubühne devotes issue to New Theatre, with
articles on Laban, with photographs.
Mary Wigman (formerly Marie Wiegmann) writes major
statement on Laban's theory of dance.

Autumn   Becomes Guest Ballet Master at Nationaltheater, Mannheim.

Dec.   Creates 'Bacchanale' in Wagner's *Tannhäuser*.
Creates *Die Geblendeten*, his first full-length abstract dance
work, with combined opera dancers and own group.
Brandenburg publishes new edition of *Der Moderne
Tanz* with additional chapter on Wigman and Laban.

1922
Feb.   Performance of *Die Geblendeten* and premiere of *Himmel und
Erde*, in Stuttgart.
Writes major statement on Festive Culture in *Die Tat* (ed
Eugen Diederichs).

June–   Holds large Summer School at Gleschendorf; creates
Sep.   *Schwingende Tempel*.
Designs, and has made, theatre and a dance studio in
Hagenbecks Tiergarten, Hamburg.
Feist opens Berlin Labanschule, and Berlin
Bewegungschöre.

Autumn   Opens Labanschule at Tiergartenstr. 2, Hamburg with
Bereska as principal collaborator.
Tanzbühne Laban formalised and moved into 'Theater am
Zoo'; rehearses new experimental works.

Dec.   Performance in Conventgarten, Hamburg of *Die Geblendeten*.
Premiere of *Der Schwingende Tempel* with Mario Volcard,
Sylvia Bodmer, Joos, Keith, Bereska, Feist as group leaders.
Premiere of *Fausts Erlösung* at Ernst Merck Halle, Hamburg,
pioneering dance with speech choir; speech directed by Vilma
Mönckeberg-Kollmar of Hamburg University.

1923
Jan.   Tanzbühne Laban performs at Deutsches Schauspielhaus,
Hamburg: solos, duos, grotesques; premiere of Bereska's solo
Orchidée.

March   Regular lecture/demonstrations in Hamburg.
Creates *Tschaikowskys Serenade* for spring festival at
Stadttheater, Rostock.

Spring   Tanzbühne Laban performs at Conventgarten, Hamburg,

with new repertory of supporting works fortnightly.
Creates *Lichtwende* as the first large choric work for amateurs.

May   Premiere of *Gaukelei*, a major dance drama, at Conventgarten, Hamburg.

Summer   Enlarges repertoire and performs widely in programmes of major works with supporting solos and duos.

Sept.   Inflation at its worst, giving severe financial problems.

Oct.   Premiere of *Komödie*, a satire, at Sagebiels, Hamburg.

Nov. 1923-March 1924 season
Creates the incidental dances for the Deutsches Schauspielhaus production of *Wintermärchen* (Shakespeare), and the dances in *Faust, Part I* (Goethe).

Dec.   Second cooperative production with Mönckeberg-Kollmar; Aeschylus's *Prometheus* for movement choir and speech choir.

1924
Jan–   Preparation for new repertory.
March   Brandenburg writes on the new art of dance in Germany.

April–   Major European tour by Tanzbühne Laban to Germany,
June   Austria, Italy and Yugoslavia, taking 1921–24 major works.
Tanzbühne Laban disbands in Zagreb for financial reasons.
Jooss and Sigurd Leeder go to Vienna; Bereska, Keith, Frank and Hildegard Troplowitz go to Rome.

June   Premiere of *Agamemnons Tod* for the Hamburger Bewegungschöre.
Publishes major statement on the concept of the movement choir.

Summer   Creates *Les Petits Riens* (to Mozart music) for Martin Gleisner's newly-formed Gera Bewegungschöre for young workers.

Movement choirs listed in the following cities:

Frankfurt	Stuttgart
Berne	Budapest
Berlin	Vienna
Lubeck	Zurich
Basle	Hamburg

Oct.   Creates incidental dances for *Sommernachstraum* (Shakespeare) at Deutsches Schauspielhaus, Hamburg.
Albrecht Knust takes over the Hamburger Bewegungschöre, with Karl Bergeest as assistant.

Nov.   Gives *Phantastische Revue* at Deutsches Schauspielhaus,
              Hamburg.
              Jooss and Leeder start Neue Tanzbühne in Munster.

1925
Jan.   Publishes major statement on Dance Theatre.

Feb.   Berliner Bewegungschöre festival, giving choric movements
              from Laban's *Lichtwende, Prometheus*, and *Agamemnons Tod*
              in the Blüthnersaal, Berlin.

Spring–   Tours as a duo with Gertrud Loeszer in musicless
Summer   programme of dances on Wagnerian characters.

Autumn   Kammertanzbühne Laban performs widely with repertoire of
              32 short works under Bereska's leadership.
              Lectures on the new art of dance.
                  Thüringer Bewegungschöre Laban is started by Martin
                  Gleisner.

Oct.   Founds nucleus of an institute for movement notation and
              research in Hamburg; main assistant Gertrud Snell.

Dec.   Creates and dances main role in *Don Juan*, a work for
              soloists and movement choir.
              Creates *Terpsichore* to Handel's score, with singer, for
              Bereska and Kammertanzbühne Laban.

1926   *Gymnastik und Tanz* published on dance education.
              Des Kindes Gymnastik und Tanz published on dance education
              for children.
              Choreographie published on choreology and notation.

Jan.   Creates *Dämmernden Rhythmen* for the Hamburger
              Bewegungschöre.

Feb.–   *Don Juan* and *Terpsichore* tour.
onwards

March   City of Würzburg invites Laban to establish a centre.

April   Verband der Laban-Schulen e.V. issues list of Labanschulen
              (21) and Bewegungschöre Laban.
                  Die Schönheit devotes two issues to Laban's work.

May–   Travels in USA for ethnographic studies; New York, Los
July   Angeles, New Mexico, Arizona, Mississippi, San Francisco.

Aug.   Summer course in Würzburg Waldkolonie, at Sternbachtal.
              Loeszer and group in residence and assisting.

Autumn	Choreographisches Institut is established in Würzburg at Theaterplatz 24, for dance notation and dance research. Aurel von Milloss is a pupil. Kammertanz Laban performances continue.
Nov.	Premiere of *Narrenspiegel* in Berlin; Laban dances 'der Narr'.
Dec.	Accident during performance of *Don Juan* at Nuremberg, which ends performance career.
1927	Teaching and lecturing in Germany, Austria and Switzerland.
Spring	Choreographisches Institut moves to Gillstr. 10, Berlin-Grunewald and expands work to include Laban Zentralschule. Assistants:

Snell	Loeszer
Eleanor Warsitz	Bereska
Susanne Babitz	Margarethe Koch
Annie Sauer	Hermann Robst

June	Premiere of *Ritterballett* for the opening of the Kurhalle at Bad Mergentheim, assisted by Bereska. Presented also at Magdeburg. Organises and leads 1st Dancers' Congress at Magdeburg, as part of the Deutsche Theater-Ausstellung. Major statement at Magdeburg on the dance as a work of art: *Das Tänzerische Kunstwerk*. Founds Tänzerbund, a union for all dancers. Premiere of *Titan* at Magdeburg, a choric work with an intermezzo for septet; assistant Margot Koch. Premiere of *Nacht* at Magdeburg, 'a dynamic materialisation', an experimental satire for large group; assistants Loeszer and Warsitz.
July	Summer School at Bad Mergentheim where major solutions to the notation are made. First dance score, of *Titan*, is written by Knust. Laban decides to publish his notation system.
Autumn	Hamburger Tanzschreibstube is started for the promotion of Laban's notation.
Nov.	*Die Tat* devotes issue to Dancers' Congress and Laban's leading role. Dr Paul Stefan publishes *Tanz in diesem Zeit*; Laban features; Laban contributes on the problems of describing a dance. Ignaz Gentges publishes *Tanz und Reigen*; Laban

contributes on 'Dance Theatre and the Movement Choir'.
Rudolf Lämmel publishes *Der Moderne Tanz*; Laban
features largely.
John Schikowski publishes *Der Neue Tanz*; chapters on
Laban and Wigman.

1928

Jan.   Continues Master Classes and examining in Labanschulen.
Titan is expanded for Hamburg celebration, at Zircus Busch.

March   *Der Scheinwerfer* publishes special issue on dance; Laban
and Jooss contribute.

Spring   Founds Deutsche Gesellschaft für Schrifttanz, a society for
the promotion of dance writing.
Gives lecture/demonstration on dance literacy illustrated by
Kammertanzbühne Laban dancers.

June   Second Dancers' Congress, organised by Jooss, in Essen.
Presents his notation system as 'Choreographie'.
Presents 'Choreologie'.
Premiere of *Grünen Clowns* with Bereska.
Musikblätter des Anbruch devotes issue to dance; Laban
contributes.

July   Founds *Schrifttanz* with editor Alfred Schlee, a scholarly
journal for the discussion of dance writing.
Laban's *Don Juan* produced at Stadtheater, Essen by
Frida Holst.
Publishes *Tanzschrift/Methodik und Orthographie*, the first
textbook on his notation.
Martin Gleisner publishes *Tanz für Alle* on Laban's
work with amateurs.

Autumn   Teaches/lectures in Halle, Brunswick, Plauen, Vienna,
Hamburg and Essen.

Oct.   Second issue of *Schrifttanz* published.

1929

Jan.   Third issue of *Schrifttanz* published; 18 notation groups are
listed.

Spring   Extensive lecture tour of main German cities, for which he
writes major statement on his fundamental concepts of dance
study, including Choreographie, Choreologie, and
Choreosophie.

Feb.   Lectures on 'Der Kampf um den Tanz'.
Gleisner publishes 'Feinde des Laientanz' in *Singchor und
Tanz*.

April–   Designs and directs *Festzug des Handwerkes und der
June   Gewerbe* for 20,000 participants in Vienna Festival

celebrations. Assistants are Fritz Klingenbeck, Gisa Gert,
Gertrud Kraus; Alfred Schlee directs music; collaborative
solo dancers are Ruth Abramowicz, Cilly Ambor, Edith Bell,
Edith Eysler, Ilse Halberstam, Maru Karjera, Olga
Suschitzky, Ellinor Tordis, Traute Witt.

May	Fourth issue of *Schrifttanz* published. Gleisner creates *Flammende Zeit* for movement and speech choir, at Social Democratic Party convention.
June	Assists Gleisner, Harry and Grete Pierenkämper to create *Alltag und Fest*, a celebratory choric work in Mannheim.
July– Aug.	Visits the Summer School in Hamburg. Runs the Summer School of Choreographisches Institut and Laban Zentralschule at Burg Lauenstein.
Aug.	Fifth issue of *Schrifttanz* published.
Sep.	Jenny Gertz teaches Kinetography in a state school in Berlin. Frankfurter Bewegungschöre Laban (directors Bodmer, Lotte Müller) in Stadtoper production of Gluck's *Orpheus und Eurydike*. Bereska opens Paris Labanschule. Financial depression begins to be felt.
Oct.	Laban Zentralschule moves to Essen to combine with Folkwanghochschule under Jooss's direction. Main assistants Leeder and Snell. Laban and Choreographisches Institut remain in Berlin, assisted by Susanne Ivers, working on dance notation and choreology.
Dec.	50th birthday celebrated at Essen. Jooss creates *Pavane* as 50th birthday present. Issue of *Singchor und Tanz* is devoted to Laban. Issue of *Der Tanz* is devoted to Laban. Sixth issue of *Schrifttanz* is devoted to Laban. Dr Werner Schuftan publishes *Handbuch des Tanzes*, for which Laban writes the Foreword.
1930	Teaching and lecturing continue.
Jan.	Frankfurter Bewegungschöre Laban at Stadtoper, Frankfurt.
Feb.	Laban's version of *Orpheus* at Staatsoper, Hamburg.
April	Jooss mounts his version of Laban's *Gaukelei* in Berlin. Hamburger Tanzschreibstube (Knust and Azra von

Laban) publishes Kinetograms.
Seventh issue of *Schrifttanz* published.

June   Laban's Deutsche Tänzerbund and Wigman's Deutsche
            Tanzgemeinschaft publish jointly innovative plans for a state
            Hochschule für Tanz.

June–   Summer Course at Bayreuth, in conjunction with Wagner
Aug.   Festival.

June   Eighth issue of *Schrifttanz* published.
            Third Dancers' Congress at Munich.
            Contributes major statement on amateur dance, from the
            cultural and educational standpoint.
                Exhibition on development of Laban's notation, in
                Munich Theatermuseum.

Aug.   Premiere of 'Bacchanale' in Wagner's *Tannhäuser* at Bayreuth
            Festival, assisted by Jooss, with dancers from the
            Choreographisches Institut and the Zentralschule Essen.

Sept.   Appointment for one year as Director of Movement at the
            State Theatres in Berlin, including Ballettmeister at Berlin
            Staatsoper Unter den Linden, following Max Terpis. Susanne
            Ivers appointed as Kinetographer.
            Choreographisches Institut moves to Folkwangschule, Essen.

Sept.–   Master Classes, lecture demonstrations and examinations at
Dec.   Folkwangschule, Essen.

Oct.   Premiere of 'Die Polowetzer Tänze' in Borodin's *Fürst Igor*;
            notated.

Nov.   Premiere of 'Walpurgis Bacchanale' in Wagner's *Margarete*;
            notated.

Dec.   Ninth issue of *Schrifttanz* published.
            Premiere of incidental dances to Wagner's *Die Meistersinger*.
            Premiere of 'Der Tanz der sieben Schleier' in R. Strauss's
            Salome.

1931
Jan.–   Continues Master Classes and examinations at Essen,
June   Folkwangschule.
            Writes on 'Sinn der Laientanzfeier' in *Tanzgemeinschaft*.
            Writes on 'Tanztheater' in *Das Prisma*.

Feb.   Premiere of incidental dances for *Eine Nacht in Venedig*
            (J. Strauss); notated.

April   Dismisses the soloists of the Staatsoper Unter den Linden,

Berlin.

June   Tenth issue of *Schrifttanz* published.

July   Revives 'Bacchanale' in Wagner's *Tannhäuser* at Bayreuth
            Festival.

Aug.   Financial depression worse.
            Snell loses job as notation teacher at Essen; joins Bereska
            in Paris.
            Movement choir festival in Hamburg with choirs from
            Mannheim, Hamburg and Berlin, and works by Knust,
            Gleisner, Pierenkämpers and Veith-Bluchel.
            Laban Tanz Studio in Berlin, run by Annemarie Dunkel
            and Edgar Frank; tours as 'Laban Tanz Studio
            Kammertanzbühne'.

Sept.   Appointment at Berlin State Theatres extended for a further
            three years.

Oct.   Last issue of *Schrifttanz*.

Dec.   Premiere of *Tänze Abende* at Schiller Theater, Berlin.
            Directs operetta *Die Geisha* at Staatsoper, Berlin.

1932   *Der Tanz* takes over *Schrifttanz*, with Knust and Gleisner
            as contributors.
            Financial depression worsens; Ivers loses job at Berlin
            Staatsoper in budget cut.
            Continues at Staatsoper, Berlin, and teaching at Essen,
            Hamburg, Paris, Berlin.

June   Member of largely classical jury at Paris International Dance
            Competition, at which Jooss takes first prize with *Der Grüne
            Tisch*; Rosalia Chladek takes second, Dorothée Günther takes
            third.

Autumn   Teaches course at Humboldt University, Berlin.

1933
Jan.   Political crisis. National Socialists take office.
            Continues at Staatsoper, Berlin, and at Essen.

June   Jury member at Warsaw International Dance Festival.

Dec.   Reichskulturkammer established; Nazification of culture
            begins.

1934   Jooss emigrates to England with company and half
            Folkwangschule dance students.

Knust takes over as director of Laban Zentralschule at Essen.
Lola Rogge takes over at Hamburg Labanschule and Bewegungschöre.

May   Reichstheaterkammer established.

June   Jury member at Vienna International Dance Competition.

July   Farewell matinée at Staatsoper, Berlin for Laban, attended by Adolf Hitler.
Leads the Summer School at Essen, with Knust and Fritz Böhme.
Chorische Tagung held, led by Marie Luise Lieschke.

Sept.   Becomes Director of newly-formed Deutsche Tanzbühne under Ministry of Propaganda, in charge of movement and dance throughout Germany. Snell main assistant, with Ivers and Richard Thum, at Potsdamerstr., Berlin.

Dec.   Runs Deutsche Tanzfestspiele in Berlin presenting out-of-work dancers, young dancers, and established names.
Premiere of *Dornröschen* given at the Festival.
Publishes *Deutsche Tanzfestspiele 1934*, writing on German Dance Theatre; other articles by Gret Palucca, Wigman and Günther.

1935   Runs classes for out-of-work dancers, promotes dance through festivals, and provincial tours. Begins organisation for international dance competition for Olympic Games, issuing invitations to leading national groups.
Knust establishes Berliner Tanzschreibstube.

May   Premiere of Laban's incidental dances in Wagner's *Rienzi* at Waldoper, Zoppot, produced by Knust from notation.

June   Power struggle within the Reichskulturkammer; Laban defends dance from takeover by R. Bode, director of gymnastics and sport.

Summer   Provincial tours of young dancers, organised by Deutsche Tanzbühne.

July   Ebrecht, Nazi Party member, put into Deutsche Tanzbühne secretariat.
Reich's regulation for dance teachers enforced.

Aug.   Directs Deutsche Tanzbühne Summer Camp for dancers at Rangsdorf. Dr Josef Goebbels visits.
Founds Reichsbund für Gemeinschaftstanz, Lieschke as

administrator, in association with Reichstheaterkammer.
Publishes *Ein Leben für den Tanz*, an autobiography.

Sept.   Reichsfachschaft Bühne for theatre founded.

Oct.   Reich theatre teachers licences introduced.
Milloss mounts Laban's *Gaukelei* at Dusseldorf.

Nov.   Second Deutsche Tanzfestspiele in Berlin, organised by
Deutsche Tanzbühne with the Reichstheaterkammer.

1936   Continues preparation for Dance events in connection with
the Olympic Games.

April   Reichsfachschaft Tanz founded, led by August Berger,
with official journal *Deutsche Tanz-Zeitschrift*.
Knust and Irmgard Bartenieff translate Feuillet into
Kinetography.

May   Appointment changes to become Director of Meisterwerkstätten für Tanz, Berlin-Charlottenburg, to direct workshops
at the highest level; Ivers, Thum, Ebrecht on staff.
Short-term staff for dance at the Olympiad only: Snell, Brice,
Meyer, Manek.

June   Runs Chortanzwoche in Berlin for many movement choirs
together.
Preview of *Vom Tauwind und der neuen Freude* at Dietrich
Eckart Freilichtbühne on the Olympic campus. Dr Goebbels
attends and forbids the performance, Rogge's *Amazonen* and
Lotte Wernicke's *Geburt der Arbeit* are allowed.

July   Runs International Dance Competition in Berlin.
Olympic Games begin.

Aug.   On holiday is interviewed by police; questionnaire on
background. Does not return to Berlin. Ivers interviewed and
job terminated. Thum's job terminated.

Nov.   Officially 'resigns' directorship of Meisterwerkstätten.

Dec.   Unofficial 'house arrest' begins at Schloss Banz.
His notation forbidden to be used.
His name not to be used in schools.
His books forbidden.

1937
Jan.–   At Schloss Banz; ill. Meisenbach, Andreas Duck assist.
Sept.

Oct.   Flees to Paris. Ill and destitute. Frances Perret assists him.

1938

Feb.   Arrives in Totnes, on a temporary visa, as guest of Jooss at
              Dartington Hall; ill.

Events in Great Britain prior to Laban's arrival

1930   Anny Fligg, Laban-trained, teaches Central European
              Dance at Chelsea PT College.

1931   Freda Colwill returns from Bodenwieser school to teach
              Central European Dance at Bedford PT College.

1932   Leslie Burrows, Wigman-trained, opens studio in London.

1933   Fligg gives recital of Central European Dance in London.

1934   Anny Boalth teaches Laban work at British Drama League.
              Joan Goodrich studies with Leslie Burrows and at Wigman
              School, Dresden (1933); returns to teach drama at Bedford
              PT College.
              Jooss/Leeder School opens at Dartington Hall; teaching
              based on Laban's concepts, notation used and taught.
              Ballets Jooss based at Dartington Hall.
              Lisa Ullmann teacher at Jooss/Leeder School.

1934   Ballets Jooss tours both internationally, and
–38   provincially in Great Britain.

1935   Ullmann starts weekly classes for amateurs for Plymouth
              WEA.
              Leeder creates and notates *Danse Macabre*.

1935   Diana Jordan studies with Wigman and 3 years with
–38   Burrows.

1936   Jooss/Leeder Summer School at Dartington Hall.

1936   Jooss/Leeder School continues.
–38   British Drama League courses continue.
              Teacher training continues at Bedford PT College.

1937   Louise Soelberg joins Burrows as teacher.

1938   Jordan publishes *Dance as Education*.
              Ann Hutchinson, advanced student at Jooss/Leeder School,
              notates *Green Table*, *Big City*, and *Pavane*.

1938

Feb–   Begins slow recovery to health. Moves to The Barton at
1939   Dartington Hall, as guest of Leonard and Dorothy Elmhirst.

Starts learning English.

Dec.   Starts writing *Choreutics*.
        Irma Otte-Betz and Bartenieff publish *Reading Studies in Laban's Dance Script* in New York.

1939   Slow recovery continues.
        Explores abstract 3-dimensional form; makes models and drawings.

July   Is given residency in UK.

Sept.   War is declared.
        Jooss/Leeder School is depleted.

1940   Slow recovery continues.

June   Devon declared a Protected Area; all aliens leave.
        With Ullmann, temporarily stays in London.
        Jooss, Leeder et al interned until Nov. 1940.

Autumn Finds refuge in Newtown, Wales, at Rock House, with Ullmann.
        Dance Notation Bureau, New York founded, by Hutchinson, Helen Priest Rogers, Henrietta Greenwood, Janey Price.

1941
Jan.   Jordan organises for Ullmann to instruct gathering of interested teachers, at Reading.

March   Jooss/Leeder school closes.

April   With Ullmann, teaches at Bedford PT College.
        PEA Annual Conference; Central European Dance taught by Betty Meredith-Jones.
        Teaches at First Conference on 'Modern Dance' at St Margaret's, Bushey, with Ullmann, Jordan, Soelberg, Goodrich, Douglas Kennedy.

Summer Ullmann teaching at St Gabriel's Teacher Training College, and at Welshpool and at Aberystwyth University.
        Gives occasional classes with Ullmann on the lawn at Rock House, Newtown.

Aug.   Laban, but mainly Ullmann, gives informal Holiday Course at Newtown.

Dec.   Appointed adviser to Paton Lawrence & Co; commutes to

Manchester on work study methods in industry.
Birmingham Education Authority appoints Soelberg to teach teachers.
Knust notator in Munich, writing Pino and Pia Mlakar's choreographies.

1942

Jan. Teaches at First Modern Dance Holiday Course with Ullmann, Goodrich, Jordan, at Moreton Hall.

Feb.– Working at Tyresoles Ltd's factory with F. C. Lawrence.
May

May 'Laban/Lawrence Industrial Rhythm' method launched.

June– Laban/Lawrence methods used for Dartington Hall Ltd, for
Aug. the sawmills, fruit packing, etc. Jean Newlove assistant.

Aug. Teaches at Second Modern Dance Holiday Course, at Moreton Hall; with Bodmer, who had come to England from Nazi harrassment.

Sept. With Ullmann moves to Manchester, 131 Palatine Road.

1943 Continues with Paton Lawrence & Co.

Jan. Teaches at Third Modern Dance Holiday Course, at Moreton Hall.
Ullmann teaches Modern Educational Dance in Manchester, for LEA teachers' course.

April Modern Dance course at Bedford, Betty Meredith-Jones.

Aug. Teaches at Fourth Modern Dance Holiday Course, at Moreton Hall.

Dec. Laban-based amateur dance groups listed in London, Birmingham, Worcester, Manchester, Doncaster, Sheffield, Wakefield, Northallerton.

1944 Continues with Paton Lawrence & Co.
Ullmann continues to expand work with teachers.

Jan. Teaches at Fifth Modern Dance Holiday Course, at Sheffield.

Aug. Teaches at Sixth Modern Dance Holiday Course, at Moreton Hall.

Sept. First Diploma Course in Dance Teaching established at Goldsmiths' College, London University, under Lilla Bauer.

Winter   Students from Dartford PT College spend 6 weeks with
            Laban and Ullmann in Manchester.
                 Tai Ai Lien notates Tibetan dances, score deposited in
                 Sinkiang Province Library.

1945   Continues with Paton Lawrence & Co.
                 Ullmann continues to expand work with teachers.

Jan.   Teaches at Seventh Modern Dance Holiday Course, at
            Sheffield.

Aug.   Teaches at Eighth Modern Dance Holiday Course, at Bishop
            Otter College.

Autumn   'Basic Movement' is established in PE as a subject, using
                 Laban's ideas.
                 Katrine Harper teaches notation in Boston Conservatory
                 Dance Department program, USA.

1946
Jan.   Teaches at Modern Dance Holiday Course, at Sheffield.
            Laban Art of Movement Guild (the 'Guild') forms; Laban is
            President.
            Art of Movement Studio (the 'Studio') opens at 108 Oxford
            Road, Manchester; Ullmann director; Laban on faculty, with
            Bodmer; 4 students.

Spring–   Continues work with Paton Lawrence & Co.
Summer   Gives lecture/demonstrations with Studio students.

Aug.   Ullmann teaches weekly at Liverpool.
                 Midlands Dance Group formed (Jordan).
            With Ullmann gives occasional classes for amateur dramatic
            clubs.

1947   Continues teaching at the Studio, now with 14 students.
            Continues work with Paton Lawrence & Co.
            Publishes *Effort* with F. C. Lawrence.

Jan.   West Riding Movement Study Circle starts (Jordan).

June   Studio students participate in International
                 Choreographic Competition at Cophenhagen with
                 Ullmann and Bodmer's *The Forest*.

Summer   Teaches at International Summer School at Interlaken;
            Wigman, Chladek, Jooss, Leeder, Harald Kreutzberg.
            Gives Presidential Address at Guild first Annual Meeting.
                 Sigurd Leeder School of Dance established in London.

Sept.
Studio larger numbers.
Kent teachers' course starts (Violet Bruce).
Emma Lugossy publishes *Hungarian Folk Dances in Kinetography*.
Hutchinson, Ullmann, Laban confer on notation development.

1948
Continues at Studio and giving lecture/demonstrations with students.
Continues at Paton Lawrence & Co, assisted by Warren Lamb and Valerie Preston.
Publishes *Modern Educational Dance*, assisted by Veronica Tyndale Biscoe.

Jan.
Guild starts twice-yearly publication of *The Laban Art of Movement Guild News Sheet* (later titled *LAMG Magazine*).

April
Guild First Annual Conference, London.
With Ullmann moves to 8 Neston Avenue, Manchester.

June
Young Dancers Group established with three senior Studio students; first performances at Library Theatre, Manchester; Bodmer directs.

Summer
With Geraldine Stephenson, teaches at British Drama League Summer Course, York.
Guild starts publishing magazine *Movement* on Laban's work.
Adda Heynssen publishes *Music for Dances* for use in Modern Educational Dance classes.

Sept.
Ministry of Education approves Art of Movement Studio 1-year course for teachers.
Students/assistants include Hettie Loman, Mary Elding, Stephenson.
Teaches as part-time faculty at Bradford Civic Playhouse Theatre School (director Esmé Church).
Produces *The Slave* at Bradford.

Nov.
Lectures on 'Motion Study in Industry' to Manchester University.

Dec.
Produces, with Esmé Church, *The Twelve Months* at Bradford.
Labanotation in curriculum of High School of Performing Arts, New York.
Doris Humphrey's *Shakers* notated.

Commencement of notating of twelve of George
Balanchine's works.

1949   Continues with Paton Lawrence & Co; at the Studio; at
Bradford Civic Playhouse Theatre School; at British Drama
League.
Continues choreological research.
Second (last) issue of *Movement* published, on Laban's
work in education.
Young Dancers Group tour.

March   Speaks on 'The Remedial Value of the Art of Movement' at a
one-day Conference in London given by the British Council
for Rehabilitation on 'Music and Art Therapy'. Here he is
introduced to Irene Champernowne of Withymead Centre for
psychotherapy.

April   Guild Easter Conference.
Article on 'Laban Movement in Therapy' published.

Aug.   Teaches at Modern Dance Holiday Course at Dartington
Hall.
Special Course for College lecturers approved by Ministry
of Education at Art of Movement Studio.

Oct.   Jooss reestablished at Folkwangschule, Essen.

Autumn   Visits Withymead three times (one visit is for 10 days).

11   Takes part in a meeting in London chaired by John
Dec.   Trevelyan 'To Discuss the Future of Art Therapy'.

Dec.   70th birthday celebrated at Studio.
Awarded 'La Plaquette d'Honneur' by Les Archives
Internationales de la Danse, by Rolf de Maré.
Publishes *Transversal 7-Rings*.
Guild Regional Groups start.

1950   Continues with Paton Lawrence & Co; at the Studio; at
Bradford; at British Drama League; and with choreology
research.
Knust begins to reestablish Kinetography Laban from
Folkwangschule Tanzschreibstube.

Aug.   Publishes *Mastery of Movement on the Stage*.
The Studio expands.
British Dance Theatre formed from Studio graduates;
Ronnie Curran, Lamb, Joan Carrington, Preston, Sally
Archbutt, Meggie Tudor; director is Loman. Tours.

With Ullmann teaches Dance Drama Course, London.
Issue of *New Era in Home and School* is devoted to
Laban's work.
Major statement on 'The Psychological Effects of Movement'
at Dartington.
Modern Dance Holiday Course, at Dartington Hall.
Teaches at American University Theatre 4-week Course at
Dartington Hall, with Ullmann; Arch Laurterer and Nadine
Miles from USA.

Dec.   British Dance Theatre TV broadcast.
Hanya Holm's *Kiss Me Kate* dances notated, score
registered for copyright in Library of Congress,
Washington DC.

1951   Continues with Paton Lawrence & Co; at Studio; at Bradford.
Assistants include Tyndale Biscoe, Beatrice Loeb, William
Ellis, Stephenson.
London Group of Guild formed; leaders Hilda Brumof,
Lilian Harmel.

March   With Ullmann teaches an Easter Course, London.

Summer   Invited to direct movement for York Mystery Plays; is ill;
Stephenson takes over.

July   Laban features as the 'Profile' in *The Observer*.

Aug.   Modern Dance Holiday Course, at Dartington Hall; new
teachers include Russell, Shiela Aste, Tyndale Biscoe;
Alec Clegg (West Riding Chief Education Officer) speaks
on 'Modern Dance in Education'.

Autumn   Juilliard School, New York opens Dance Department;
Labanotation required subject.
Jooss returns to direct Folkwangschule Tanzabteilung,
Essen.
Knust's Institut der Kinetographie established at
Folkwangschule.
Kinetographie Laban taught in Hungarian State Ballet
School, Budapest, by Lugossy.

Winter   Leads London Weekend Courses on 'Choral Dance Drama'
with Ullmann.
Merseyside Guild regional group started.
Kiss me Kate musical, Hanya Holm choreog, comes to
London as a notated score; Ann Hutchinson assists
reconstruction at the Coliseum.

1952 Continues with Paton Lawrence & Co; at the Studio; at Bradford.

Jan. With Ullmann, teaches on Christmas Holiday Course.
Guild publishes booklet *The Art of Movement in Education, Industry and the Stage.*
Yorkshire regional group started.
British Dance Theatre tours (1951–52).

Feb. Gives Presidential Address at Guild Conference on 'Art, Education and Work'.
Gives the first Laban Lecture on 'The Art of Movement in the School' for the Guild.

March Guild Affiliated Groups start.

April Teaches on Easter Holiday Course with Ullmann.

July Second German Dance Conference, Recklinghausen; Wigman, Jooss, Kreutzberg, Marianne Vogelsang, Dora Hoyer, Knust represent Laban's influence.

Aug. Remounts *Swinging Cathedral* (1922) with Ullmann and Bodmer at Modern Dance Holiday Course, at Eastbourne.

Oct. Lamb, Carrington lecture to psychiatrists on effort assessment and personal efficiency.
Guild publishes 2nd edition of booklet *The Art of Movement in Education, Work and Recreation.*
Journal of Mental Science states 'Laban Movement is in psychotherapy'.
The Ministry of Education publishes *Moving and Growing*, a major policy statement on movement education in state schooling.
First post-war International Kinetography Conference at Essen; Knust, Hutchinson, Preston.

1953
Spring– Hospitalised with Typoid Fever.
Summer

Feb. Guild Annual Conference; Ullmann.

Summer Preliminary work on book 'Effort and Recovery' (never completed).

Aug. Studio moves to new rural premises at Woburn Place, Addlestone, donated by William Elmhirst. Faculty is Laban, Ullmann, Stephenson, Marion North, Preston.
Attends Modern Dance Holiday Course, at Ashridge.

Guild Professional Members' Course; Ullmann, Bodmer teach.

Dance Notation Record, quarterly of the Dance Notation Bureau, starts.

Nadia Chilkovsky publishes *3 R's for Dancing in Labanotation*.

Autumn   Begins collaboration with William Carpenter on theoretical analysis of movement in relation to Jungian theory.

1954   Teaches occasionally at Studio and outside. Private therapeutic work with individuals.

Researches with Studio faculty as assistants: Preston for notation and choreutics, North for effort and recovery, all for choreology with educational themes.

Writes Foreword for Hutchinson's *Labanotation*.

Feb.   Gives Laban Lecture on 'The Art of Movement' for Guild Annual Conference.

March   Writes 'Letter to Guild Members' as major statement of his philosophy.

Easter   Leads course for men with Ullmann and Graeme Bentham.

Aug.   Lecture/demonstration and men's classes at Modern Dance Holiday Course, Ashridge.

Guild Professional Members' Course; Ullmann, Bodmer, North.

Oct.   *Scope: Magazine for Industry* publishes article on Laban.

Dec.   75th birthday celebrated—by performance at Toynbee Hall of British Dance Theatre (Loman and Archbutt) and Stephenson.

Ninette de Valois embraces Labanotation, but switches to system devised by member of Royal Ballet (Benesh).

Hutchinson publishes *Labanotation*.

1955   Continues with teaching occasionally at Studio and outside; with therapeutic consultancy; and with research with Studio faculty as assistants.

Guild regional groups and local dance circles active, especially Manchester, West Riding and London.

Overseas College and University Dance Departments become affiliated to Guild.

The Laban Art of Movement Centre is established as research counterpart to educational work of the Studio; Laban is director.

Feb. Gives Laban Lecture at Guild Annual Conference on 'Recreation, Research, Rehabilitation'.

March Creates with Ullmann *Saltata* with Bizet's *L'Arlesienne Suite* for Festival of Dance at Wembley Pool, with 200 performers.

Autumn Assists Ullmann in London Evening Classes with North. Gives 12-week course on 'Psychological Implications of Movement' at Addlestone with North.

Winter With Ullmann teaches at London Weekend Courses, 'Choral Dance Plays'.
　　　　Discussions between Hutchinson and Leeder on development of notation.

1956 Concentrates on research work at LAM Centre. Continues therapeutic consultancy. North assists on manuscript of 'Effort and Recovery', and of 'Movement Portraits', part of Youth Advice Bureau. Publishes *Principles of Dance and Movement Notation,* assisted by Preston. Writes Vorwort for Knust's *Abriss der Kinetographie Laban.*

Feb. Gives Laban Lecture at Guild Conference, on 'Dance Culture'.

Aug. Lectures on 'Dance Mime and Dance Drama' at Modern Dance Holiday Course, Ashridge.

Oct. Teaches with Ullmann and Bodmer at Guild Course for Professional Members.

Autumn Commences consultancy to Arts in Industry project with North at factory of Walter Wears.
　　　　Ruth Morrison publishes *Educational Gymnastics* in which Laban's influence on gymnastics teaching methods and criteria are evident.
　　　　Knust publishes *Abriss der Kinetographie.*
　　　　Labanotation accepted as a credit at Bennington College, Vermont.
　　　　Reconstruction from the score of Balanchine's *Symphony in C* (1st movement) for School of Performing Arts concert.
　　　　Imperial Society of Teachers of Dance publish their Stage syllabus written in Labanotation.
　　　　Dance Notation Bureau publish Ted Shawn's *16 Dances in 16 Rhythms.*
　　　　Nadia Chilkovsky writes *10 Dances in Labanotation.*

Reconstruction of Humphrey's *Shakers* at UCLA.
12 US school/college departments offer courses in
Labanotation by qualified teachers.

1957   Continues research/writing as in 1956.

Feb.   Gives Laban Lecture at Guild Conference, on 'Caring for
Movement'.

April   Lectures on 'Education through the Arts' at Royal Festival
Hall for Society for Education through Art.

July   Lectures at Third Congress of International Association for PE
for Girls and Women, in London.

Summer   Ill.
Modern Dance Holiday Course held at Ashridge.

Oct.   Ullmann talks in East Germany on Kinetography.
International Congress on Folk Dance Research, in
Dresden, adopts Kinetography as official research system.

Dec.   Teaches/receives factory employees of Arts in Industry
project, who perform dance version of *Amahl and the Night
Visitors*, dedicated to him.
Russell publishes a textbook for teachers, *Modern Dance
in Education*.
Dance Notation Bureau publishes book on ballroom
dancing in Labanotation.
Gertrude Kurath notates American Indian dances.
Hutchinson lectures on 'Dance Notation Systems' at
University College, Oxford.
Bauer and Preston give lecture/demonstration on dance
notation for the British Association of Organisers and
Lecturers in PE.
Cecchetti Council adopts Labanotation as its official
system.
Hutchinson lectures on notation to the Physical
Education Association; Preston demonstrates.

1958   Continues research and writing.

Feb.   Gives Laban Lecture 'The World of Rhythm and Harmony'
—a major statement on the spiritual element.

May   Gives paper 'Movement concerns the whole man'—a major
statement of holistic philosophy, at Council for Education
through Art, with Ullmann and North.

Summer   Diana Baddeley, Ingeborg Baier commence courses in

Kinetography in Poland, at the Folklore Institute,
Warsaw, with Roderyk Lange.
Knust teaches in USA: Philadelphia, New York, Jacob's
Pillow, and Connecticut College.

July   Dies on the 1st; is buried in Weybridge, Surrey.
Meg Abbie starts teaching Labanotation in Australia.
Els Grelinger notates *My Fair Lady* (Holm) in New
York.
Baddeley teaches notation at École Supérieur D'Études
Choreographiques, Paris.
Knust publishes English translation of *Abriss der
Kinetographie* as *Handbook of Kinetography Laban*.

14 A chronology of Rudolf Laban's dance works

This chronology of dance works illustrates Laban's wide output and range of styles, subject and scale. Full-length works and short solos are all included. English translations of titles have been given and beneath each is a statement of genre which, wherever possible, is a quotation from Laban himself. The titles indicate his interest in myth, in the universal idea, and in dances about movement itself. The words 'dance works' are used, not the more customary 'choreographies', because Laban's output included choric works, pageants, revues, dance dramas and a 'dynamic realisation'. These differences run into each other and defy categorisation.

Laban was sole choreographer for the majority of works and so only the names of collaborators are shown in the chronology on the next few pages. For many works Laban created or organised the sound and therefore only the names of other people creating sound/music are listed. Similarly, for many works Laban designed his own costumes, and there was no scenery; only known collaborators are therefore stated.

Premiere	Title/kind	Collaborators for: choreography (ch) sound (s)/music (m) design (d)	Performers	Venue
Summer 1903 or 1904	La fête du tigre (Festival of the Tiger) 'A light-hearted play'		Ad hoc group of amateurs	Nice
Autumn 1912	Die Erde (parts only) (The Earth) A 'Tanz Mysterium', (mystery play for dance in 5 Reigen)		Ad hoc group; Maja Lederer, singer	Atelier für Tanz und Bewegungs-kunst, Munich
Summer 1913	Tanzende Trommelstock (The Dancing Drumstick) A sequence of rhythmical dances		Summer School participants, including Wiegmann and Perrottet	Monte Verità, Ascona
Summer 1913	Ishtars Höllenfahrt (Ishtar's Journey Into Hades) 'A myth'		Summer School participants, including Wiegmann and Perrottet	Monte Verrità, Ascona
23 January 1914	Im Hain des Aeskulap (In the Grove of Aesculapius)		Wiegmann, Perrottet, Weysel doctors, nurses, dancers from	Munich

Date	Work	Performers / Notes	Location
	Carnival celebration	the Laban de Varalja Schule für 'Tanz, Ton, Wort'	
End January 1914	*Walhallball* (*Valhalla Ball*) Carnival celebration for the Munich press	Weigmann, Perrottet, Weysel, dancers, from the Laban de Varalja Schule für 'Tanz, Ton, Wort'	Munich
February 1914	*Die Geburt des Tanzes in der Hölle* (*The Birth of the Dance in Hell*) Carnival celebration	Wiegmann, Perrottet, Weysel, dancers from the Laban de Varalja Schule für 'Tanz, Ton, Wort'	Munich
July 1914	*Sieg des Opfers* (*Victory of Sacrifice*) (rehearsal only)	scenario and libretto Hans Brandenburg / Leistikow, Wiegmann, Falke sisters, Oesterreich, Wulff, Perrottet, Mohr	Monte Verità, Ascona (Intended for the Trades Exhibition, Cologne 1914)
Mid-April 1916	*Der Spielmann* (*The Fiddler*) Dance with a story	Laban school students with Wiegmann	Kaufleuten, Zurich
18/19 August 1917	*Die Sang an die Sonne* (*The Song to the Sun*) Dance hymn in 3 Reigen	Wiegmann, Perrottet, Mohr, Weysel, Bereska and participants in the O.T.O. masonic festival	Monte Verità on 3 outdoor locations, Ascona (Performed at sun-set, midnight and dawn)

22 August 1917	*Die Wunderblumen* (*The Miraculous Flowers*) 'A fairy tale'		Soloists and group	Monte Verità, Ascona
1918	*Der Grimasse des Sultans* (*The Sultan's Grimace*)		Perrottet, Wulff, Bereska and students	Schule der Bewegungskunst, Zurich
4 December 1921	'Bacchanale' in *Tannhäuser* (Nordic version)	m Wagner	Resident Opera dancers and Tanzbühne Laban	Nationaltheater, Mannheim
20 December 1921	*Erste Epische Tanzfolge* (*First Dance Symphony*) Abstract choric dance (also known as *Die Geblendeten* (*The Deluded*) and *Schwingende Gewalten* (*Swinging Powers*))	m with Freidrich Wilckens, partly silent	Resident Opera dancers and Tanzbühne Laban	Nationaltheater, Mannheim
20 December 1921	*El fenreigen* (*Elfin Reigen*), males; and *Sylphentanz* (*Dance of Sylphs*), females	m Berlioz		Nationaltheater, Mannheim
20 December 1921	*Ungar Marsch* (*Hungarians' March*)			Nationaltheater, Mannheim

Date	Work	Music/notes	Company	Theatre
20 February 1922	*Himmel und Erde* (*Heaven and Earth*) Tragi-comic pantomime (also known as *Oben und Unten* (*Above and Below*))	m with Wilckens	Jooss, Bereska, Knust, Algo, Smalova and Tanzbühne Laban	Württembergisches Landestheater, Stuttgart
20 February 1922	*Ur Rhythmen* (*Primeval Rhythms*)			Württembergisches Landestheater, Stuttgart
14 December 1922	*Fausts Erlösung* (*Faust's Salvation*) Choric dances with choric speech	s Goethe's *Faust Part II*; speech direction Vilma Mönckeberg-Kollmar	Tanzbühne Laban and Hamburger Bewegungschöre; Hamburger Sprechchor	Ernst Merck Halle, Hamburg
18 December 1922	*Der Schwingende Tempel* (*The Swinging Cathedral*)	m with Wilckens	Tanzbühne Laban	Conventgarten, Hamburg
5 March 1923	*Tschaikovskys Serenade*	m Tchaikovsky	Tanzbühne Laban	Stadttheater, Rostock
April 1923	*Elegie* (*Elegy*)		Roon	Oldenburg
April 1923	*Orchidée* (*The Orchid*)	ch with Bereska	Bereska	Oldenburg

Date	Title		Performers	Location
April 1923	*Männertanz* (*Men's Dance*) from *Erste Epische Tanzfolge*		Laban, Frank, Keith, Jooss	Oldenburg
15 May 1923	*Zaubergarten* (*Magic Garden*) A fairy tale	ch with Bereska	Kammertanzbühne Laban	Theater am Zoo, Hamburg
May 1923	Tanzbühne Laban repertoire of supporting works—classification by Laban in publicity is shown beneath title			Theater am Zoo, Hamburg
	Ballade Ornamental		Quartet	
	Bizarrer Zweitanz (*Bizarre Duo*) Grotesque		Laban and Jooss	
	Dreimännertanz (*Trio for Men*) Rhythmic		Frank, Jooss, Keith	
	Magyarischen Klange (*Magyar Sounds*) Style dance			
	Schattenwegs (*Shadow Paths*) Grotesque		Duo for men	

Date	Work	Music	Performers	Venue
	Schwank (*Tottering*) Grotesque			
	Spruheufel (*Firework*) Grotesque			
	Sostenuto Ornamental		Bereska	
24 May 1923	*Lichtwende* (*Dawning Light*) A work for movement choir	s Laban (percussion score, played by dancers)	Hamburger Bewegungschöre	Conventgarten (Grosse Saal), Hamburg
29 May 1923	*Gaukelei* (*Illusions*) A dance drama		Tanzbühne Laban	Conventgarten (Grosse Saal), Hamburg
July 1923	Tanzbühne Laban supporting works added:			Württemburgisches Landestheater, Stuttgart
	Kyclops (*Cyclops*) Grotesque		Jooss	
	Raumgespinst (*Spatial Weave*) Ornamental		Group	

			Group	
6 September 1923	*Slavischen Rhythmen* (*Slavonic Rhythms*) Style dance	ch with Bereska s silent	Kammertanzbühne Laban	Theater am Zoo, Hamburg
2 October 1923	*Die Drachentöterei* (*The Dragon Slayer*) A fairy tale; a 'Tanzscherz' (mimetic joke)		Tanzbühne Laban	Sagebiel, Hamburg
November 1923	*Komödie* (*Comedy*) 'A dancing matter in 4 Reigen'		Tanzbühne Laban soloists with Schauspielhaus cast	Deutsches Schau-spielhaus, Hamburg
10 December 1923	Incidental Dances for *Wintermärchen* (*A Winter's Tale*—Shakespeare)	s percussion words Aeschylus speech direction Mönckeberg-Kollmar	Tanzbühne Laban soloists, Hamburger Bewegungschöre, Hamburger Sprechchor	Ernst Merck Halle, Hamburg
February 1924	*Prometheus* (*Prometheus*) (also known as *Gefesselte Prometheus* (*Prometheus Bound*)) Tanzbühne Laban supporting works for European tour:			Theater am Zoo, Hamburg

Aufschwung (*Impulse*)	
Choral (*Chorale*)	
Fünfvariationen (*Five Variations*)	Bereska
Groteske (*Grotesque*)	
Gruppentanz (*Group Dance*)	Kammertanzbühne Laban
Klagelied (*Lament*)	Kammertanzbühne Laban
Nocturne	
Orchestische Gespräche (*Orchestic Conversations*)	Gertrud Loeszer
Raumrhythmen (*Spatial Rhythms*)	Loeszer
Risolute *Resolute*	
Schemen (*Silhouettes*)	

Date	*Tanz* (Dance)		Performers	Place
March	*Basso Ostenato*		Hildegard Troplowitz	Berlin
	Bewegtes Thema (*Moving Theme*)		Gerda Scheck	
	Gobesches Thema		Jens Keith	
	Gruppengroteske (*Group Grotesque*)		Tanzbühne Laban	
	Männer Tanz II (*Men's Dance II*)		Kammertanzbühne Laban men	
	Phantasmagorie (*Spookiness*)		Loeszer	
	Stiltanz (*Style Dance*)		Gerd Neggo	
24 June 1924	*Agamemnons Tod* (*Death of Agamemnon*) Dramatic movement choir	s percussion score	Kammertanzbühne Laban soloists, Hamburger Bewegungschöre	Sagebiel, Hamburg
1924	Incidental Dances for *Josephslegende*	m R. Strauss producer Kroeller	Mario Volcard, Bereska	Staatsoper, Hamburg
1924	Incidental Dances to Goethe's *Faust Part I*		Kammertanzbühne soloists and Schauspielhaus cast	Deutsches Schauspielhaus, Hamburg

		ch after Noverre m Mozart		
Autumn 1924	*Les Petits Riens*	ch after Noverre m Mozart	Jena and Gera movement choirs	Unknown
October 1924	Incidental Dances to *Sommernachtstraum* (*A Midsummer Night's Dream*—Shakespeare)		Kammertanzbühne soloists and Schauspielhaus cast Hamburg	Deutsches Schauspielhaus, Hamburg
November 1924	*Phantastische Revue/Wachsfiguren Kabinett in 12 Bilden* (*Fantastic Review/Waxworks in 12 Scenes* A burlesque review		Kammertanzbühne Laban	Deutsches Schauspielhaus, Hamburg
January 1925	*Orchestik* Programme of dance works		Kammertanzbühne Laban, Hamburger Bewegungschöre	Volksoper, Hamburg

Repertoire prepared for the Kammertanzbühne Laban's 1925 season:

	Alte Tanzvisionen (*Vision of Ancient Dances*) Style dance		Solo: Bereska; duo: Bereska, Hermann Robst	Theater am Zoo, Hamburg
	Arabesken (*A suite of solos, duos, trios*) Ornamental		Kammertanzbühne	

Bauerntänze (*Peasant Dances*) Style dance	Kammertanzbühne
Begegnung (*Encounter*) Rhythmical	Motta Nolling, Robst
Burleske Gigua and *Walzerparodie* Humorous	Kammertanzbühne
Byzanz Ecstatic	Laban, Bereska; plus Robst
Chinesenstadt (*Chinese City*) Stylised	Robst
Dithyrambus (*Dithyramb*) Rhythmical, 'a choric poem in praise of Dyonysius; inspired, irregular, exalted, impassioned'	Laban, Robst
Furlefanz (*Fooling Around*) Grotesque	Robst

Formate (*Forms*) Rhythmical	Laban
Das Grauen (*Horror*)	Group
Homunkulus (*The Artificial Man*) Grotesque	Laban
Icosaeder (*Icosahedron*) Ornamental	Snell
Ifriti Rhythmical	Laban, Robst
Im Lande des Schweigens (*In the Land of Silence*)	Kammertanzbühne
?!(Interpunktionstanz) (*Punctuation Dance*) Grotesque, 'frivolous, hindrances, uncompleted moves, stoppages	Bereska
Ipanema Rhythmical	Robst

Irwische (*Will o' the Wisp*) Grotesque	Jüngling, Berner
Klub der Sonderlinge (*Cranks' Club*) Grotesque	Quartet
Kreuzgänge (*Cloisters*) Ornamental	Women's group
Krystall (*Crystal*) Ornamental	Bereska
Lustleid (*Joy/Grief*) Ecstatic	Bereska, Laban
Marotte (*Quirk*) Grotesque, 'comic'	Laban
Marsch Rhythmical	Quartet
Der Mönch (*The Monk*) Ecstatic	Laban

Mondänes (*The Chic Thing*) Grotesque			Laban	
Phantastisches Kabarett (*Fantastic Cabaret*)			Kammertanzbühne	
Rhythmische Suite (*Rhythmical Suite*) Rhythmical			Kammertanzbühne	
Rituale und Opfertänze (*Ritual and Sacrificial Dances*) Ecstatic			Laban, Bereska	
Rosetten (*Rosettes*) Ornamental			Bereska	
Träume (*Dreams*) Ecstatic			Group	
Troll				
4 December 1925 *Terpsichore* A ballet	ch with Bereska m Handel, arr Woelffers		Kammertanzbühne Laban, solo Bereska	Hamburg

Date	Work	Notes	Company	Venue
4 December 1925	*Don Juan* A dance drama	m Gluck	Kammertanzbühne Laban, movement choir	Hamburg
24 January 1926	*Dämmernde Rhythmen* (*Dawning Rhythms*) Choric dance poem	ch with Albrecht Knust s percussion score: with Edgar Neiger	Hamburger Bewegungschöre	Thalia Theater, Hamburg
April/May	*Choreographische Tänze* Choreographed (ie notated) dances on Wagnerian characters	s silent	Laban and Loeszer	Unknown
2 November 1926	*Westliche Contemporains* (untranslatable)	ch with Bereska	Kammertanzbühne Laban	Pfauentheater, Zurich
17 November 1926	*Narrenspiegel* (*Fool's Mirror*) Dance ballade	ch with Bereska m Liszt	Kammertanzbühne Laban	Neues Theater am Zoo, Berlin
12 June 1927	*Ritterballett* (*Ballet of the Knights*) Dance work in 4 Reigen	m Beethoven d Hans Blanke	Kammertanzbühne Laban, Choreographisches Institut dancers	Kurhalle, Bad Mergentheim
17 June 1927	*Titan* Choral work	m Rudolf Wagner-Régeny on percussion score by Laban; and Beethoven d Blanke	Tanzbühne Laban, Choreographisches Insitut dancers	Stadthalle, Magdeburg

Date	Work	Credits	Performers	Venue
18 June 1927	*Nacht* (*Night*) 'Dynamic materialisation in a prologue and 13 scenes'	s Erich Itor Khan; percussion score Laban d Blanke	Kammertanzbühne Laban, Choreographisches Institut dancers	Stadthalle, Magdeburg
1927	*Orpheus*	m Gluck	Soloists, and movement choir	Unknown
23 June 1928	*Grünen Clowns* (*Green Clowns*) 'A grotesque in 6 movements'	ch with Bereska m Itor Khan	Kammertanzbühne Laban, Choreographisches Institut dancers	Stadtheater, Essen
9 June 1929	*Festzug des Handwerkes und der Gewerbe* (*Pageant of Craft and Trade*) Series of dances celebrating craftsmanship	direction Laban assisted by Fritz Klingenbeck, Gisa Geert, Gertrud Kraus m Max Brand, Julius Bittner, Ernst Krenek, Egon Wellesz; director Alfred Schlee d floats and costumes Laban	Massed members of Guilds of Viennese Crafts; solo dancers Ruth Abramovitz, Cilly Ambor, Edith Bell, Edith Eylser, Ilse Halberstam, Maru Karjera, Olga Suschitzky, Ellinor Tordis, Traute Witt	Ringstrasse, Vienna

Date	Work			Venue
23 June 1929	*Alltag und Fest* (*Everyday and Festival*) A choric celebration	ch with Martin Gleisner s speech choir, text Martin Gleisner	Movement choirs from Jena, Gera, Frankfurt, Mannheim, etc; solo speaker Martin Gleisner	Sportstadion, Mannheim
9 August 1930	'Bacchanale' in *Tannhäuser* (Paris version)	ch assisted by Kurt Jooss m Wagner direction S. Wagner, Toscanini	70 dancers	Festspielhaus, Bayreuth
11 October 1930	'Polowetzer Tänze' in *Fürst Igor* (Polovstian Dances in *Prince Igor*)	kinetograms Susanne Ivers m Borodin	Staatsoper Unter den Linden	Staatsoper Unter den Linden, Berlin
12 November 1930	'Walpurgisnacht Bacchanale' in *Margarete* (Faust)	m Gounod	Staatsoper Unter den Linden	Staatsoper Unter den Linden, Berlin
November/December 1930	'Der Tanz der sieben Schleier' in *Salome* ('Dance of the Seven Veils' in *Salome*)	m R. Strauss	Staatsoper Unter den Linden	Staatsoper Unter den Linden, Berlin
November/December 1930	Incidental Dances for *Die Meistersinger von Nürnberg*	m Wagner	Staatsoper Unter den Linden	Staatsoper Unter den Linden, Berlin

Date	Work	Credits	Performers	Venue
20 February 1931	Incidental Dances for *Eine Nacht in Venedig* (*Night in Venice*)	kinetograms Ivers m J. Strauss, arr E. Korngold	Staatsoper Unter den Linden	Staatsoper Unter den Linden, Berlin
25 December 1931	*Tänze* (*Dances*) Incidental dances and production of dancers		Staatsoper dancers	Schiller Theater, Berlin
30 December 1931	*Die Geisha* (*The Geisha*)	kinetograms Susanne Ivers m Sidney Jones	Staatsoper Unter den Linden	Staatsoper Unter den Linden, Berlin
16 December 1934	*Dornröschen* (*Sleeping Beauty*) A ballet	m J. Strauss, arr Leo Spiess costumes and set Laban	Staatsoper Unter den Linden	Staatsoper Unter den Linden, Berlin
22 May 1934	Incidental Dances for *Rienzi*	kinetograms Albrecht Knust m Wagner	Deutsche Tanzbühne group	Waldoper, Zoppot
20 June 1936	*Vom Tauwind und der neuen Freude* (*The Warm Wind and the New Joy*) Choric celebration (preview only)	m Hans Klaus Lange words from Nietzsche	Movement choirs from 21 cities	Dietrich Eckart Freilichtbühne, Berlin

15 Writings by Rudolf Laban: A chronological list

'Symbole des Tanzes und Tanz als Symbol' ('Symbols of dance and dance as symbol'), *Die Tat* (December 1919), pp. 669–675.

'Kultische Bildung im Feste' ('Religious education in festival'), *Die Tat* (June 1920), pp. 161–168.

Die Welt des Tänzers (*The Dancer's World*), (Walter Seifert Verlag, Stuttgart, 1920, third edition, 1926).

'Die Bewegungskunst und das neue Theater' ('The art of movement and the new theatre'), *Die Fahne* (January 1921), pp. 14–19.

'Eurhythmie und Rakorhythmie in Kunst und Erziehung' ('Eurhythmy and "Rakorhythmie" in art and education'), *Die Tat* (May 1921), pp. 137–139.

'Der moderne Tanz' ('The modern dance'), *Die Tat* (February 1922).

'Festwille und Festkultur' ('Desire for festival and culture of festival'), *Die Tat* (February 1922), pp. 846–848.

'Aus einem Gespräch über das Tanztheater' ('From a discussion about dance theatre'), *Die Tat* (December 1922), pp. 676–680.

'Die Erneuerung in der Bewegungsregie des Theaters' ('Renewal in the directing of movement in the theatre'), *Hamburger Anzeiger* (19 May 1923).

'Tanzformen' ('Dance forms'), *Die Rampe*, Magazine of Deutsches Schauspielhaus, Hamburg (Season 1924/25, 1 November).

'Vom Geist des Tanzes' ('The spirit of dance'), *Die Rampe*, Magazine of Deutsches Schauspielhaus, Hamburg (Season 1924/25, 1 November).

'Der Tanz und die neue Generation' ('Dance and the new generation'), *Die Freude* (September 1925), pp. 398–402.

'Der Tanz als Eigenkunst' ('Dance as an art in itself'), *Zeitschrift für Äesthetik und Allgemeine Kunstwissenschaft* (1925), pp. 356–364.

Choreographische Abende (*Choreographic Evenings*) (booklet, 1925).

'Tanztheater und Tanztempel' ('Dance theatre and dance temple'), *Die Schönheit* (Heft 1, 1926), pp. 42–48.

'Das Tanztheater' ('The dance theatre'), *Die Schönheit* (Heft 1, 1926, *Appendix*), pp. 3–4.

'Plagiat in Tanz und Gymnastik' ('Plagiarism in dance and

gymnastics'), *Die Schönheit* (Heft 2, 1926, *Appendix*), pp. 19-20.

'Vom Sinn der Bewegungschöre' ('The idea of movement choirs'), *Die Schönheit* (Heft 2, 1926), pp. 84–91.

Choreographie: Erstes Heft (Choreography: First Volume) (Eugen Diederichs, Jena, 1926).

Gymnastik und Tanz (Gymnastics and Dance) (Gerhard Stalling Verlag, Oldenburg, 1926).

Des Kindes Gymnastik und Tanz (Gymnastics and Dance for the Child) (Gerhard Stalling Verlag, Oldenburg, 1926).

'Geist und Form des Tanzes' ('Spirit and form of dance'), *Der Tanz* (November 1927), pp. 2–5.

'Das tänzerische Kunstwerk/oder: Wie es leiben und leben sollte' ('The dance art work/or: how it should be to a T'), *Die Tat* (November 1927), pp. 588–591.

'Tanztheater und Bewegungschor' ('Dance theatre and movement choir'), *Tanz und Reigen*, ed. I. Gentges (Bühnenvolksbund-verlag, Berlin, 1927), pp. 72–79.

'Vortragsbezeichnungen und Bewegungsbegriffe' ('Performance expressions and movement terms'), *Tanz in dieser Zeit*, ed. P. Stefan (Universal-Edition, Vienna, 1927), pp. 25–28.

'Choreographie und Theater' ('Choreography and theatre'), *Der Scheinwerfer* (March 1928), p. 22.

'Tanzschrift und Schrifttanz' ('Dance notation and written dance') (June 1928), Laban Coll: 205.07-.09.

'Zwei Äusserungen zum II. Deutschen Tänzerkongress' ('Two comments on the IInd German Dancers' Congress'), with V. Skoronel, *West-Woche* (June 1928), pp. 10–11.

'Grundprinzipien der Bewegungsschrift' ('Basic principles of movement notation'), *Schrifttanz* (July 1928), pp. 4–5.

'Tanzkomposition und Schrifttanz' ('Dance composition and written dance'), *Schrifttanz* (October 1928), pp. 19–20.

'Die Entwicklung der Bewegungsschrift Laban' ('The development of the Laban movement notation'), *Schrifttanz* (October 1928), pp. 27–30.

'Vom Tanzinhalt' ('The content of dance'), *Der Tanz* (November 1928), pp. 2–3.

'Das chorische Kunstwerk' ('The choral art work'), *Singchor und Tanz* (Heft 12, 1928), pp. 160–161.

'Choreographie und Theater' ('Choreography and theatre'), *Der Scheinwerfer* (Heft 11/12, 1928), p. 22.

Schrifttanz: Methodik, Orthographie, Erläuterungen (Written dance: Methodology, Orthography, Explanations) (Universal-

Edition, Vienna, 1928, English and French editions, 1930).
There is no indication on the face of these publications that
Laban was the author.

'An die deutsche Tänzerschaft' ('To the German dance
community'), *Der Sturm* (No.19, 1928/29), pp. 258–260.

'Die Erneuerung in der Bewegungsregie des Theaters' ('Renewal
in the directing of movement in the theatre'), *Singchor und Tanz*
(15 January 1929), pp. 18–19.

'Probleme des Tanzes' ('Problems of dance'), *Schrifttanz* (January
1929), p. 19.

'Rhythmus der Jugend 1929' ('Rhythm of youth 1929'), in the
booklet *Jubilaeumswoche des Nationaltheaters* (Mannheim, June
1929), pp. 21–22.

'Über die tänzerischen Berufe' ('The dance professions'), *Der Tanz*
(December 1929), pp. 2–4.

'Das Choreographische Institut Laban' ('The Laban Choreo-
graphic Institute'), *Monographien der Ausbildungsschulen für
Tanz und tänzerische Körperbildung, Band I, Berlin*, ed. L.
Freund (Leo Alterthum Verlag, Berlin, 1929), pp. 11–14.

'Aufgaben und Möglichkeiten der Tanzschrift' ('Aims and possibilities of dance notation'), *Jahrbuch des Tanzes 1929*, pp.
196–198.

'Vom Sinn der Bewegungschöre' ('The idea of movement choirs'),
Schrifttanz (June 1930), pp. 25–26.

'Anna Pawlowa' ('Anna Pavlova'), *Schrifttanz* (June 1930), pp.
8–9.

'Vom Geist des Tanzes' ('The spirit of dance'), *Singchor und Tanz*
(15 June 1930), pp. 179–180.

'Sinn der Leientanzfeier' ('The idea of an amateur dance festival'),
Tanzgemeinschaft (No. 3, 1930), p. 5.

*Schrifttanz: Kleine Tänze mit Vorübungen (Written Dance: Short
Dances with Preliminary Exercises)* (Universal-Edition, Vienna,
1930, text in German, English and French). There is no
indication on the face of this publication that Laban is the author.

'Das Tanztheater' ('Dance theater'), *Das Prisma* (Vereinigten
Stadttheater Duisburg-Bochum, Heft 14, 1930–31), pp.
133–136.

'Neue Tanzkunst' ('The new art of dance'), *Magdeburger
Tageszeitung* (8 December 1934).

*Deutsche Tanzfestspiele 1934 unter Förderung der
Reichskulturkammer (German Dance Festival 1934 Promoted by
the National Chamber of Culture)*, ed. R. Laban (Carl Reissner

Verlag, Dresden, 1934).

'Die deutsche Tanzbühne' ('The "Deutsche Tanzbühne" '), *Deutsche Tanzfestspiele 1934 unter Förderung der Reichskulturkammer* (Carl Reissner Verlag, Dresden, 1934), pp. 3–7.

'Deutsche Tanz' ('German dance'), *Singchor und Tanz* (1934).

Ein Leben für den Tanz (Carl Reissner Verlag, Dresden, 1935); (translated 1975 as *A Life for Dance*, see below).

'Meister und Werk in der Tanzkunst' ('Master and work in the art of dance'), *Deutsche Tanz-Zeitschrift* (May 1936), pp. 1–4.

'Entstehung und Entwicklung des Gemeinschaftstanzes' ('Origin and development of community dance'), *Die Westmark* (August 1936), pp. 608–609.

'Die deutsche Tanzbühne' ('The "Deutsche Tanzbühne" '), *Die tänzerische Situation unserer Zeit* (Carl Reissner Verlag, Dresden, 1936), pp. 3–7.

Choreutics (Part I written in 1939, see also 1966 below).

Laban/Lawrence Industrial Rhythm and Lilt in Labour, with F. C. Lawrence (Paton Lawrence & Co, Manchester, 1942).

Effort, with F. C. Lawrence (Macdonald & Evans, London, 1947).

'The President's Address at the AGM of the LAMG', 27 August 1947 (on the breadth of his vision of the art of movement), *LAMG News Sheet* (No. 1, January 1948).

Message of good wishes to first issue, in *Movement* (Summer 1948) p. 3.

Modern Educational Dance (Macdonald & Evans, London, 1948); 2nd edition revised by Ullmann, L. (*ibid.*, 1963); 3rd edition revised and enlarged by Ullmann, L. (*ibid.*, 1975) (reissued by Northcote House, Plymouth, 1988).

'The Key to the Space Harmony of Movement' sent out by Laban at Christmas 1949.

Mastery of Movement on the Stage (Macdonald & Evans, London, 1950); 2nd edition revised by Ullmann, L. as *The Mastery of Movement* (*ibid.*, 1960); 4th edition revised and enlarged by Ullmann, L. as *The Mastery of Movement (ibid.*, 1980) (reissued by Northcote House, Plymouth, 1988).

'What has led you to study movement? (answered by R. Laban)', *LAMG News Sheet* (No. 7, September 1951).

'Presidential Address at the AGM of the LAMG', 1952 (on Art, Education, and Work), *LAMG News Sheet* (No. 8, March 1952).

'The Art of Movement in the School' (given at the Annual Guild Conference 1952), *LAMG News Sheet* (No. 8, March 1952).

'The Work of the Art of Movement Studio', *Journal of Physical Education* (Vol. 46, No. 137, 1954), pp. 22–30.

'A Letter to Guild Members', *LAMG Magazine* (No. 12, March 1954), pp. 5–9.

'The Art of Movement' (The Laban Lecture, 1954, primarily on choreosophic concerns), reported by his secretary D. Bond in *LAMG Magazine* (No. 12, March 1954), p. 22.

'Foreword by Rudolf Laban', *Labanotation*, Hutchinson, A. (Theater Arts, New York, 2nd edition, 1970), pp. xiii–xvi (written by Laban in 1954).

'Letter to Guild Members', *LAMG Magazine* (No. 14, March 1955), pp. 4–9.

'The Three Rs of the Art of Movement Practice' (The Laban Lecture, 1955), *LAMG Magazine* (No. 14, March 1955).

'From Rudolf Laban's Early Writings' (English translations of notes made by Laban which later formed the basis of *Ein Leben für den Tanz* (1935)), *LAMG Magazine* (No. 15, October 1955).

'Movement' (The Laban Lecture, 1956), *LAMG Magazine* (No. 16, March 1956).

Principles of Dance and Movement Notation (Macdonald & Evans, London, 1956); 2nd edition issued as *Laban's Principles of Dance and Movement Notation (ibid.,* 1975).

'Vorwort' (Foreword), *Abriss der Kinetographie Laban*, Knust A. (Das Tanzarchiv Verlag, Essen, 1956), pp. ix–xi.

'Movement, an Art and a Philosophy' (The Laban Lecture, 1957), *LAMG Magazine* (No. 18, March 1957).

'Education through the Arts', *LAMG Magazine* (No. 19, November 1957), p. 4.

'The Objective Observation of Subjective Movement and Action' (lecture given at the International Congress of Physical Education for Women), *LAMG Magazine* (No. 19, November 1957).

'The World of Rhythm and Harmony' (The Laban Lecture, 1958), *LAMG Magazine* (No. 20, March 1958), p. 6.

Published posthumously

'Movement as an Integrator, (i) Movement Concerns the Whole Man' (talk given on behalf of LAMG at Whitsun Conference 1958 held at National Film Theatre by the Joint Council for Education through Art), *LAMG Magazine* (No. 21, November 1958).

A collection of his writings, as a tribute:

'The Importance of Dancing' (The Laban Lecture);

'The Educational and Therapeutic Value of Dance';
'Meaning';
'Dance and Symbol';
'The Aesthetic Approach to the Art of Dancing';
'Dance as a Discipline';
'The Rhythm of Living Energy';
all in *LAMG Magazine* (No. 22, May 1959).

'The Rhythm and Effort of Recovery, Part I', *LAMG Magazine* (No. 23, November 1959).

'The Rhythm and Effort of Recovery, Part II', *LAMG Magazine* (No. 24, May 1960).

'Light—Darkness', *LAMG Magazine (No. 25, November 1960).*

'Dance in General', *LAMG Magazine* (No. 26, May 1961).

Choreutics, ed. L. Ullmann (Macdonald & Evans, London, 1966).

'Extract from an Address held by Mr Laban on a meeting for Community Dance in 1936', *LAMG Magazine* (No. 52, May 1974).

A Life for Dance, trans. and ed. L. Ullmann (Macdonald & Evans, London, 1975, see also *Ein Leben für den Tanz*, 1935).

Gleisner, M. 'Conversations between Laban and myself', *LAMG Magazine* (No. 65, November 1980).

'Man Agog', *LAMG Magazine* (No. 67, November 1981).

'Notes on Movement Therapy', *LAMG Magazine* (No. 71, November 1983).

A Vision of Dynamic Space, compiled by L. Ullmann (Falmer Press, in association with Laban Archives, London, 1984).

16 Persons mentioned in the texts and their relationship to Laban

Abbie, Meg	Labanotation teacher, Australia
Abramovitz, Ruth	Dancer, Vienna Festzug
Algo, Julian	Dancer in the Tanzbühne Laban
Ambor, Cilly	Dancer, Vienna Festzug
Archbutt, Sally	Bedford and AMS trained; dancer
Aste, Sheila	AMS student; dance educator
Babitz, Susanne	Assistant, Choreographisches Institut
Baddeley, Diana	AMS trained; Knust's notation assistant, Folkwangschule 1950s
Baier, Ingeborg	Notator, East Berlin
Barker, Clive	Actor with Joan Littlewood
Bartenieff, Irmgard	Laban-trained; pioneer of notation and Effort/Shape in USA; pioneer of dance therapy; writer
Bauer, Lilla	Ballets Jooss company member; teacher of dance, Goldsmiths' College
Bell, Edith	Dancer, Vienna Festzug
Bentham, Graeme	AMS student/assistant
Bereska, Dussia Feldt	Laban's major assistant 1919–1929. Co-director of Kammertanzbühne Laban; co-choreographer of many works
Bergeest, Karl	Tanzbühne Laban dancer; assistant Hamburger Bewegungschöre
Berner, Gretl	Kammertanzbühne Laban dancer
Blank, Hans	Designer for 1927 Laban works
Boalth, Anny	Laban-trained teacher at British Drama League and RADA
Bode, Rudolf	Leader of one kind of body culture in Germany
Bodmer, Sylvia	Soloist in Tanzbühne Laban. Co-leader Frankfurter Bewegungschöre Rudolf von Laban. Teacher AMS; collaborator in Modern Dance Holiday Courses; Artistic Director Manchester Dance Circle 1943–1989
Böhme, Fritz	Dance historian and writer

Brandenberg, Hans Dance writer, friend in Munich, librettist of
   Sieg des Opfers

Browne, Martin Formerly Director of British Drama League,
   director of York Mystery Plays

Bruce, Violet Dance educator

Brumhof, Hilda Laban student; ballet mistress

Burger, August Leader of Fachschaft Tanz of the
   Reichstheaterkammer

Burrows, Leslie Mary Wigman student; Director of Burrows
   studio in London

Carpenter, William Collaborator on proposed book in 1954

Carrington, Joan Bedford and AMS trained; dancer; dance
   teacher

Champernowne, Director of Withymead Centre for
   Irene psychotherapy

Chase, Marion Dance therapy pioneer

Chilkovsky, Nadia Notator in Philadelphia; dance educator

Chladek, Rosalia Dance teacher and choreographer in Dalcroze
   tradition

Church, Esmé Director of Bradford Civic Playhouse
   Theatre School

Clegg, Alec Education Officer, supporter of Laban's
   work

Colville, Freda Dance teacher, Bedford College of PT

Curran, Ronnie AMS trained; dancer

Dalcroze, Emil Teacher; innovator of the Eurhythmics
   Jacques system of music/movement education

Delsarte, Francois Teacher; voice and movement theorist;
   Laban encountered his system in Paris

Diederichs, Eugen Publisher. Editor of *Die Tat*.

Duck, Andreas Schoolteacher at Lichtenfels; friend at
   Schloss Banz 1936

Dunkel, Annemarie Co-director Laban Tanz Studio, Berlin

Ebrecht, A. Nazi party member in Deutsche Tanzbühne
   Berlin office

Elding, Mary AMS student, Manchester; artist

Ellis, C. D. Paton Lawrence & Co; collaborator in
   Laban/Lawrence Industrial Rhythm

Elmhirst, Dorothy Philanthropist; owner and director of
   Dartington Hall

Elmhirst, Leonard	ditto
Elmhirst, William	Philanthropist; AMS student
Espenak, Lilian	Wigman student, developer of dance therapy
Eysler, Edith	Dancer, Vienna Festzug
Falke, Grete	Solo dancer, student at Ascona 1914
Falke, Ursula	ditto
Feist, Herta (*also* Hertha)	Tanzbühne Laban soloist; Laban School and movement choir leader, Berlin
Feuillet	Dance theorist and creator of 'Chorégraphie', which Laban developed into his own Kinetography
Fligg, Anny	Central European Dance teacher in UK in 1930s
Forsythe, William	Choreographer of the Frankfurst Ballet, using choreutics in his compositional method
Frank, Edgar	Tanzbühne Laban soloist; co-director Laban Tanz Studio, Berlin
Fricke, Martha	Laban's first wife, a painter
Garrard, Alan and Wiles, John	Authors and teachers of drama
Gentges, Ignaz	Author
Gert, Gisa	Assistant, Vienna Festzug
Gertz, Jenny	Dance educator; movement choir leader for children
Gleisner, Martin	Leader Thüringer Bewegungschöre; promoter of dance for all; author
Goebbels, Josef	Reich Minister of Propaganda, under whom Laban worked
Goodrich, Joan	Wigman/Burrows trained; dance teacher Bedford College of PT
Graf, Oskar	Writer; visitor to Monte Verità
Greenwood, Henrietta	Co-founder, Dance Notation Bureau, New York
Grelinger, Els	Notator, USA
Gross, Otto	Asconian psychiatrist
Grotowski, Jerzy	Polish theatre director and theorist
Günther, Dorothée	Director of Günther School, Munich; choreographer; movement choir director
Halberstam, Ilse	Dancer, Vienna Festzug

Harmel, Lilian	Laban student; dance teacher
Hitler, Adolf	Führer and Reichskanzler
Holm, Hanya	Teacher; choreographer; Wigman-trained; founder-director of Hanya Holm Studio, New York
Holst, Frida	Ballet mistress, Essen
Hoyer, Dora	Ausdruckstänzerin
Hutchinson, Ann	Jooss/Leeder-trained; co-founder Dance Notation Bureau, New York; major figure in Labanotation in USA and UK; author and notator
Itor Khan, Erich	Composer and Musical Director in 1927 and 1928
Ivers, Susanne	Notator at Berlin State Opera; administrative assistant in Deutsche Tanzbühne and Meisterwerkstätten für Tanz
Joos, Khadven	(*see* Jooss, Kurt)
Jooss, Kurt (*previously* Joos, Khadven)	Tanzbühne Laban soloist; collaborator in formation of Kinetography Laban; director of Zentralschule Laban; founder/director of Ballets Jooss, and of Jooss/Leeder School at Dartington
Jordan, Diana	Burrows-trained; dance educator; collaborator Modern Dance Holiday Courses; founder of West Riding Movement Study Group; founder member of Laban Art of Movement Guild
Jüngling, Else	Kammertanzbühne Laban dancer
Karjera	Dancer, Vienna Festzug
Keith, Jens	Tanzbühne Laban soloist
Kennedy, Douglas	Founder-director English Folk Song and Dance Society
Kestenberg, Judith	Movement therapy pioneer using Laban's ideas
Klingenbeck, Fritz	Dancer; assistant, Vienna Festzug; assistant at Choreographisches Institut; collaborator on notation; writer
Knust, Albrecht	Tanzbühne Laban soloist; major collaborator in formation, development and promotion of Kinetography Laban; leader of

	Hamburger Bewegungschöre; Director of Zentralschule Laban; founder of Hamburger Tanzschreibstube
Koch, Margarethe	Assistant at Choreographisches Institut
Kraus, Gertrud	Assistant, Vienna Festzug
Kreutzberg, Harald	Solo dancer/choreographer
Kurath, Gertrude	Ethnochoreologist in USA
Laban, Azra von	Laban's daughter; assistant, Hamburger Tanzschreibstube
Lämmel, Rudolf	Author
Lamb, Warren	AMS student; assistant for individual work; pioneer of Effort/Shape; author
Lange, Hans Klaus	Composer for *Tauwind* 1936
Lange, Roderyk	Ethnochoreologist, Poland
Lawrence, D. H.	Novelist; visitor to Monte Verità
Lawrence, F. C.	Management consultant; collaborator in Laban/Lawrence Industrial Rhythm; co-author of *Effort*; co-founder of Laban Art of Movement Guild
Lederer, Maja	Laban's second wife; a singer; mother of five of his children
Leeder, Sigurd	Performer and collaborator in Ballets Jooss; co-director of Jooss/Leeder School, Dartington; collaborator on the formation and development of Kinetography; director Sigurd Leeder School of Dance, London
Leistikow, Gertrud	Actress; collaborator in Brandenburg's *Sieg des Opfers*
Lieschke, Marie Luise	Community dance administrator
Littlewood, Joan	Theatre director, friend in Manchester
Loeb, Beatrice	Choreographisches Institut student; supporter of Laban's work
Loeszer, Gertrud (*sometimes* Loeser *or* Loesser)	Kammertanzbühne Laban dancer; teacher, Choreographisches Institut
Loman, Hettie	AMS trained; choreographer; founder of British Dance Theatre
Louis, Murray	Choreographer; collaborator of Nikolais
Lugossy, Emma	Hungarian dance teacher and notator

Malmgren, Yat	Student of Laban; movement teacher and play director
Maré, Rolf de	Director of Les Archives Internationales de la Danse
Maudrik, Lizzie	Ballet mistress, Berlin
Meier, Walli	Nonington and AMS student; specialist on recreative and special education
Meisenbach, Jo	Pupil and associate of the Munich period; friend in 1936 at Banz
Melvin, Murray	Actor, with Joan Littlewood
Mensendieck, Bess	A leader of one kind of medically-based body culture of the Weimar period
Meredith-Jones, Betty	Laban/Ullmann student assistant in Newtown; dance teacher at Homerton College
Milloss, Aurel von (*also* Milloss, Aurelio)	Student at Choreographisches Institut; ballet master; major proponent of Laban's work in the theatre
Mlakar, Pia	Choreographisches Institut student; joint ballet master, Munich
Mlakar, Pino	ditto
Mönckeberg-Kollmar, Vilma	Director Hamburger Sprechchor; lecturer at Hamburg University
Mohr, Ernst	Student and dancer at Ascona and Zurich
Morrison, Ruth	Pioneer of Educational Gymnastics
Müller, Lotte	Co-director Frankfurter Bewegungschöre
Neggo, Gerd	Kammertanzbühne Laban dancer
Neiger, Edgar	Cooperating percussionist for *Dämmernde Rhythmen*
Newlove, Jean	Assistant for Laban/Lawrence Industrial Rhythm; movement teacher at Theatre Workshop
Nikolais, Alwin	Ballet Director; pupil of Hanya Holm and later her assistant
Nolling, Motta	Kammertanzbühne dancer
North, Marion	St Gabriel's and AMS trained; AMS assistant and teacher; pioneer in Personality Assessment
Obrist, Hermann	Painter and applied artist; teacher of Laban in Munich in 1899; friend/confidant

Oedenkoven, Henri	Founder of the Monte Verità settlement
Oesterreich, Laura	Dancer at Ascona
Otte-Betz, Irma	Notation teacher
Palucca, Gret	Solo dancer/choreographer
Pavlova, Anna	Prima ballerina; Laban wrote an appreciation of her artistry on her death
Perrottet, Suzanne	Dalcroze teacher; Laban collaborator, especially of the 1913–17 period; leader of the Laban School in Zurich
Peters, Kurt	Hamburg School trained; dance archivist
Pierenkämper, Grete	Co-leader of Mannheimer Bewegungschöre
Pierenkämper, Harry	ditto
Plowright, Joan	Actress; student AMS
Preston, Valerie	AMS student; assistant for notation and choreutics; dancer; teacher at AMS
Price, Janey	Co-founder Dance Notation Bureau, New York
Priest Rogers, Helen	ditto
Ranson, Malcolm	Bretton Hall trained; fights director
Robst, Hermann	Kammertanzbühne Laban dancer; assistant, Choreographisches Institut
Rogge, Lola	Director of Hamburg Labanschule and Hamburger Bewegungschöre after Knust; choreographer
Roon	Tanzbühne Laban dancer
Russell, Joan	AMS trained; dance educator
Sauer, Annie	Assistant, Choreographisches Institut
Scase, David	Theatre director
Scheck, Gerda	Kammertanzbühne Laban dancer
Schikowski, John	Author
Schlee, Alfred	Editor of *Schrifttanz*; writer
Schlemmer, Oscar	Bauhaus teacher; experimenter in dance
Schmidt, Margarethe	Laban dance teacher
Schönlanke, Bruno	Socialist poet; collaborator with Martin Gleisner
Schoop, Trudi	Wigman student; developer of dance therapy

Schuftan, Werner	Author
Sherborne, Veronica	Bedford and AMS student; assistant for *Modern Educational Dance*; pioneer of methods for handicapped children
Smalova, E.	Tanzbühne Laban dancer
Snell, Gertrud	Notation assistant at Choreographisches Institut; administrative assistant at Deutsche Tanzbühne and Meisterwerkstätten für Tanz
Soelberg, Louise	Dancer with Ballets Jooss; co-teacher with Burrows; founder Birmingham Contemporary Dance Club
Stanislavsky	Russian actor and theorist
Stefan, Paul	Author
Stephenson, Geraldine	Bedford and AMS student; assistant at Bradford Civic Playhouse Theatre School; teacher AMS; solo dancer and choreographer
Suschitsky, Olga	Dancer, Vienna Festzug
Szentpal, Maria	Ethnochoreologist in Hungary
Tai Ai Lin	Jooss/Leeder student; dancer, teacher and notator in China
Täuber, Sophie	Student in Ascona and Zurich; painter, Dadaist, married to Hans Arp
Terpis, Max	Pupil of Perrottet and Wigman; ballet master, Berlin
Thum, Richard	Dancer; administrative assistant with Deutsche Tanzbühne
Tordis, Ellinor	Dancer, Vienna Festzug
Toscanini, Arturo	Orchestral conductor; conductor at the Bayreuth Festival
Trevelyan, John	Educationalist
Troplowitz, Hildegard	Tanzbühne Laban dancer
Tudor, Meggie	AMS-trained dancer
Tyndale Biscoe, Veronica	Bedford and AMS student; dance educator; pioneer of dance with the handicapped
Ullmann, Lisa	Laban Diploma from Lotte Wedekind School; teacher at Jooss/Leeder School; major collaborator 1938–58; director of AMS

Veith-Bluchel, J.	Hamburger Bewegungschöre member
Vogelsang, Mariane	Ausdruckstanz teacher
Volcard, Mario	Tanzbühne Laban soloist
Wagner, Siegfried	Richard Wagner's son; opera director at Bayreuth
Wagner-Régeny, Rudolf	Musical director and composer for *Titan*
Walther, Clara	Student in Zurich, Dada participant
Warsitz, Eleanor	Assistant at Choreographisches Institut
Wellesz, Egon	Composer for the Vienna Festzug
Wernicke, Lotte	Dance teacher and choreographer
Weysel, Karl	Painter; Laban student at Ascona, Munich and Zurich; first partner of Mary Wigman
Wiegmann, Marie (*see* Wigman, Mary)	
Wigman, Mary (*previously* Wiegmann, Marie)	Dancer; teacher; choreographer; studied music with Dalcroze before training with Laban; Laban master student 1913; collaborator 1914–18; leading artist of the New German Dance
Wilckens, Friedrich	Musical director and composer for Tanzbühne Laban
Witt, Traute	Dancer, Vienna Festzug
Wulff, Käthe (*also* Käte)	Student at Ascona and Zurich, leader of a Laban School in Basel until 1988

17 Principal archive collections

The **Laban Collection** is a working collection of documents, video and audio tapes, and photographs brought together since 1984 to form a resource for students and scholars. It contains copies of all the major documents of the period directly relating to Laban, concentrating on the 1900–42 period. It is supported by the Gulbenkian Foundation. The Laban Centre specialist dance library contains many of the dance journals and magazines since 1940 where references can be found to Laban's work.

John Hodgson's Private Laban Collection contains several original Laban costume designs, posters, programmes, cartoons and photographs from the early period; numerous newscuttings of reviews and material related to Laban activities; articles, books and translations, and transparencies, together with recorded interviews conducted with Laban's fellow workers and associates throughout Europe and USA.

The **Laban Archive** is a collection of the material left by Laban to Lisa Ullmann and additions collected by her. This archive is now in the process of being catalogued. The **National Resource Centre for Dance** also contains more recent material relating to Laban's activities in the UK.

The **Dartington Hall Records** contain the correspondence between the administration of Dartington Hall, Dorothy and Leonard Elmhirst, and Lisa Ullmann and Laban, and official documents, amongst them complete documentation of the Elmhirsts' work. The period 1938–42 is covered, and some letters up to 1953 are available.

The **Deutsches Tanzarchiv Köln** contains a full collection of German dance magazines and newspapers of the 1920s and 30s, together with much other dance material not immediately connected with Laban. Several contemporaries of Laban have left their personal collections to this archive. It was the private collection of Kurt Peters, and is now in the possession of the city of Cologne.

The **Mary Wigman Archiv**, not all of which is available to the public, is her personal collection of documents and material on her career. Her time with Laban (1913–19) is included, and her professional relationship with him throughout her life is evident in the materials.

The collection at the **Tanzarchiv der DDR** was documented by Kurt Peterman and is a particularly rich holding of dance writings of the Weimar and Third Reich periods. Not all their materials are yet catalogued.

Knust left his personal archive to Roderyk Lange, who has catalogued and protected it. It is particularly rich in early Kinetography scores and in letters and teaching materials, as well as documentation of the Hamburger Bewegungschöre.

Grete Müller has created an archive on the materials in the possession of **Sigurd Leeder** at his last school in Herisau. It is rich in photographic material and documents relating to his schools and his method.

The **Archive of Labanotation Scores** held by the Dance Notation Bureau contains the largest collection of notation scores, ranging from some of the first written in the USA to recent additions.

The **Kurt Jooss Achiv** contains materials which give a clear account of his life, work and works, including his early contact with Laban. His daughter, Ana Markard, holds the notated scores of four of his works.

Several personal collections exist, not open to the public, held by members of the Laban family. Photocopies of much of these personal holdings have been kindly made available to the Laban Collection at the Laban Centre in London.

Other principal libraries and museums have holdings which can provide resources for study, such as the Dance Collection at the New York Public Library, the archive of the Berlin State Opera Unter den Linden, the Paris Opera archive, and the Vienna Theatre Museum. University and city libraries all over Germany, in Zurich, Vienna, Budapest, London, and in the USA can all provide resources but these cannot be listed here.

The Laban Collection	The Laban Centre for Movement and Dance, Laurie Grove, New Cross, London, SE14 6NH.
John Hodgson's Private Laban Collection	Performance Arts Faculty, Bretton Hall, West Bretton, Wakefield, West Yorks, WF4 4LG.
The Laban Archive	National Resource Centre for Dance,

	University of Surrey, Guildford, Surrey, GU2 5XH.
Dartington Hall Records	Dartington Hall, Totnes, Devon.
Deutsches Tanzarchiv Köln (formerly Kurt Peters Archiv)	Suddelratherstrasse 247, 5000 Köln 30, Germany.
Mary Wigman Archiv	Akademie der Kunst (Darstellende Kunst), Hanseatenweg 10, 1 Berlin 21, Germany.
Tanzarchiv der DDR	Akademie der Künste der DDR, Gottscheidstrasse 16, 70-10 Leipzig, Germany.
Albrecht Knust Collection	c/o Dr Roderyk Lange, Centre for Dance Studies, Les Bois, St Peter's, Jersey, Channel Islands.
Sigurd Leeder Archiv	c/o Grete Müller, Mühlebühl 16a, Herisau, Switzerland.
Archive of Labanotation Scores	Dance Notation Bureau, 31 West 21st Street, New York, NY 10010, USA.
Kurt Jooss Archiv	Uhlandstr. 7, 6200 Wiesbaden, Germany.

18 Laban Schools and their Directors in 1927

This list (given in a publicity pamphlet issued by Verband der Labanschulen EV, Berlin) illustrates how Laban handled the education of dancers. His schools proliferated and he needed to establish and maintain standards, which he did by setting up an examination system. The Laban Diploma was awarded only by an examination personally conducted by Laban after training in a Laban School, usually for three years. The Diploma was revalidated each year, by attendance at his Summer School at which the new concepts and practice of choreology were taught and examined.

In this way his continuing developments in choreutics, eukinetics and kinetography were passed on to practising teachers. He was troubled by unscrupulous teachers who set up schools in his name without being able to teach his work adequately. His article on plagiarism (1929) is a complaint on this subject. To meet this, he initiated the Verband der Labanschulen EV, an association to which registration was only available to teachers with accreditation. Here he distinguished between those with a full Diploma, and those in the process of getting the Diploma but allowed to teach in his name. Registration carried with it the obligation on the school's part to pay Laban a royalty, and on his part to carry out examinations and to visit from time to time, usually once a month, to give master classes.

Notice that some schools and movement choirs were operated by the same leader. Some choirs had sufficient training in their regular meetings to be regarded as schools (*see* Jena and Leipzig). The word *Gymnastik* has to be understood as meaning exercise or technique training, and *Tanz* as expressive work with clear artistic content. ('(Dipl.)' indicates 'Diplomlehrer der Bewegungslehre Laban'.)

Aachen	Gymnastikschule und Bewegungschor Lilian Artner
Basel	Laban-Schule Käte Wulff (Dipl.)
Berlin	Tanz-u. Gymnastikschule Hertha Feist (Dipl.) Berliner Bewegungschöre Laban. Leitung: Martin Gleisner (Dipl.)

	Gymnastikschule u. Bewegungschor Berthold Schmidt
	Berliner Labanschule Lotte Wedekind (Dipl.)
Braunschweig	Ingeborg Ramien, Schule f. Tanz u. Gymnastik
Breslau	Labanschule Gerti Heyn
Darmstadt	Wilma Hofmann, Schule f. Tanz u. Gymnastik
Esslingen a.N.	Schule für Tänzerische Gymnastik Gretel Berner
Frankfurt a.M.	Schule für Tanz und Gymnastik Sylvia Bodmer (Dipl.), Lotte Müller (Dipl.)
	Schule für Tanz und Gymnastik Hedwig Steger
Hamburg	Bewegungschor Jenny Gertz (Dipl.)
	Hamburger Bewegungschöre Rudolf von Laban. Leitung: Albrecht Knust (Dipl.)
	Schule für Tanz und Gymnastik Senta Pander
Hannover	Gymnastikschule and Bewegungschor Trude Einecke-Bosse
Jena	Thüringer Bewegungschöre Rudolf von Laban. Leitung: Martin Gleisner (Dipl.)
Kiel	Unterrichtsstätte für Gymnastik und Tanz Margarete Hahn
Köln	Ausbildungsstätte für Tanz und Gymnastik Lies Eisinger (Dipl.), Emita Torök (Dipl.)
Leipzig	Sächsische Bewegungschöre Rudolf von Laban. Leitung: Sophie Nahnsen (Dipl.)
München	Tanz-und Gymnastikschule Elisabeth Lang-Corret (Dipl.)
Nordhausen a.H.	Schule für Tanz u. Gymnastik Hilde Nebelung-Naumann
Nürnberg	Schule für Tanz und Gymnastik Herta Meisenbach
Potsdam	Potsdamer Bewegungschöre Botjo Markoff
Prag	Milca Mayerowa, Schule f. Tanz u. Gymnastik.
Wiesbaden	Schule f. Tanz u. Gymnastik Wilma Hofmann
Zürich	Bewegungsschule Suzanne Perrottet

19 Laban Movement Choirs established by 1924

By 1924 twelve choirs had started. This list appeared on the back of the programme for Laban's *Agamemnons Tod*, premiered in Hamburg on 24 June 1924. The choirs were a form of dance organisation for men and women amateurs created by Laban to fulfil the basic need of everyone to participate in celebratory events through artistic means. For them a new genre of work was created, first by Laban and later by the choir leaders with his guidance. The need for notation was paramount for such an event, for choirs rehearsed in their own city from a score and then came together for the festive performance.

It is significant that the choirs were 'of the Tanzbühne', Laban's professional company. He saw choirs and company as one entity, and made works where both performed together. Thus a choric work for soloists and choir could be performed by the Tanzbühne soloists in one city's choir and repeated with another city's choir. No doubt Laban had the established practice of cantata performances in mind as a model.

Bewegungschöre der Tanzbühne Laban
sind eingerichtet in:

HAMBURG
Leitung: Albrecht Knust

BERLIN
Leitung: Herta Feist

WIEN
Leitung: Margarete Schmidts

LÜBECK
Leitung: Senta Pander-Gellmitz

FRANKFURT a. M.
Leitung: Sylvia Bodmer, Lotte Müller

STUTTGART
Leitung: Edith Walcher

MÜNSTER i. W.
Leitung: Kurt Jooss

GERA, Reuss
Leitung: Martin Gleisner

ZÜRICH
Leitung: Susanne Perrottet

BERN
Leitung: Emmi Sauerbeck

BASEL
Leitung: Käte Wulff

BUDAPEST
Leitung: Emita Török

Auskünfte durch die Tanzbühne Laban, Hamburg,
Tiergartenstrasse 2

20 Movement choirs participating in 'Tauwind', 1936

These movement choirs were mentioned in the programme for the preview of *Vom Tauwind und der neuen Freude* in 1936. *Tauwind*, Laban's last work in Germany, was created by him and notated by Knust, not in all details but sufficiently to form a practical working tool to enable rehearsals to take place in separate towns, with minimum time alloted for final communal rehearsals in the theatre. In this respect it was a unique occurence.

The piece was created to Beethoven's *9th Symphony* and rehearsed to that music. A new orchestral score was written by Hans Klaus Lange for the performance itself, played by the Rundfunk (Radio) Orchestra. The number of movement choirs had increased since the 1924 list, giving a cast of 2,000 participants, and it was according to contemporary sources 'an architectural and uplifting work', celebrating human spiritual endeavour. It was created for a prestigious event, the inauguration of the Dietrich Eckart open-air theatre on the monumental Olympic Games campus. The preview, before an invited audience, was attended by the highest officer of the Nazi State Chamber for Culture, Dr Josef Goebbels. He wrote in his diary:

> Rehearsal of festival dance work: freely based on Nietzsche, a bad, contrived and affected piece. I forbid a great deal. It is all so intellectual. I do not like it. That is because it is dressed up in our clothes and has nothing whatever to do with us.

The work was never performed for the opening ceremony of the theatre, and Laban was stripped of his position as Director of the 'Master Workshops in Dance', deprived of a living, his books and his notation forbidden and his name erased from German culture. Such was the fate meted out by Nazism to those who did not celebrate the State and the Führer according to party dictates.

Die Tanzgemeinschaften:

aus

Baden-Baden   Irma Fink
Berlin   Hertha Feist
    Helene Grimm-Reiter

	Dodo Hagen
	Irene Hennig
	Jutta Klamt
	Angela Kutzke
	Stephanie Schmidt-Pelckmann
	Berty Rieser
	Edith Skopnik
	Berthe Trümpy
	Rita Vollmer
	Eva Schaube
	Lotte Wernicke
Brandenburg	Ingeborg Kroeker
Braunschweig	Susanne Kabitz
Bremerhaven	Friedrich Meier-Homberg
Dresden	Gert Fritsche, Ingeborg Gönnert (Palucca Schule)
Düsseldorf	Lucie Wientz
Erlangen	Carla Schlichthaar
Frankfurt/Main	Lotte Müller
Hamburg	Lola Rogge
Hannover	Tonia Wojtek
Heidelberg	Margot Andreae
Ibbenbüren	Ida Beermann
Kiel	Hann Hass
Köln	Maria Schallenberg
Magdeburg	Lilly Böttger-Heyde
Mannheim	Lotte Troelsch, Grete und Harry Pierenkämper
Müllheim (auch Bochum, Essen, Duisburg)	Heide Woog
München	Dorothee Günther
Nürnberg	Greta Wrage von Pustau
Oberursel	Jean Krieger
Remscheid	Nora von Delius
Saarbrücken	Jo Telesch
Stuttgart	Grete Breitkreuz, Brita Stegmann

21 Schrifttanz representatives by May 1929

The Society for Written Dance (Schrifttanz) was a support, promotion and teaching organisation for Laban's newly-presented dance and movement notation system. They sponsored the journal *Schrifttanz* which, while starting as a notation-orientated publication, developed into the first serious journal for the discussion of all kinds of dance writings at a scholarly level. These lists show the contacts Laban had for his notation, and how he organised its promotion through establishing individual representatives all over Germany, with the beginnings of a foreign network, too. The central organ for notation was the Hamburg-based Dance Notation Centre, under Albrecht Knust's leadership.

The world financial crisis and unemployment of 1929–31, felt strongly in Germany, had repercussions on notation. Two vital people lost their jobs, notator Susanne Ivers at the Berlin State Opera, and Gertrud Snell, notation teacher at the Laban Central School at the Folkwangschule, Essen. The journal *Schrifttanz* was crippled and taken over in 1932 by the more popular magazine *Der Tanz*. The political crisis of 1933 also seriously disrupted notation, for Sigurd Leeder and Kurt Jooss, two of Laban's main collaborators on the notation, emigrated through Nazi harassment. Knust found himself working in isolation. He had to take over the Essen school, and divide his attention between notation and dance training. Finally in 1936 the notation was forbidden by the government, along with all Laban's work.

List of local representatives for the Deutsche Gesellschaft für Schrifttanz in 'Schrifttanz' October 1928:

Berlin	Dr Ewald Moll
Aachen	Lilian Artner
Altenburg in Sachsen	Oskar Guhlmann
Altona-Bahrenfeld	Lola Rogge
Braunschweig	Ingeborg Ramien
Breslau	Gerti Hein

Chemnitz in Sachsen	Dr Julius Trübsch
Darmstadt	Wilma Hoffmann
Düsseldorf	Lucie Wientz
Essen	Dr Hanna Mendel
Esslingen	Gretl Berner
Frankfurt a. M.	Sylvia Bodmer
Halle a. S.	Jenny Gertz
Hamburg	Albrecht Knust
Hannover	Trude Einecke-Bosse
Jena	Hildegard Grebe-Grottewitz
Kiel	Margarete Hahn
Köln	Lies Eisinger
Köslin i. P.	Helene Pikron
Leipzig	Ottar Witow
Lübeck	Paul Lühr
München	Elisabeth Lang-Corret
Nordhausen a. H.	Hilde Nebelung-Naumann
Nürnberg	Herta Meisenbach
Plauen i. V.	Dr Gottfried Lieschke
Stuttgart	Richard Thumm

In Österreich:
Wien	Käthe von Hye

In der Schweiz:
Basel	Käthe Wulff
Zürich	Suzanne Perrottet

In U.S.A.:
New York	Frau Otte-Betz
Berkeley	Annie Mundstock-Heilbuth

In Frankreich:
Paris	Marguerite Debrie

In Holland:
Amersfoort	Line Tiggers

In der Tschechoslowakei:
Prag	Milca Mayerowa

In Ungarn:
Budapest	Lilly Kallay

In Jugoslawien:

Zagreb	Elisabeth von Törne

In Lettland

Libau	Ilse Loesch
Riga	Gertrud Bosse

New local groups listed in 'Schrifttanz' January 1929:

Annaberg	Elisabeth Horn
Brünn (C.S.R.)	Peter Schorck
Bamberg	Verlagsbuchhändler Meisenbach
Duisburg	Gottfried Herbers
Dresden	Sekretariat der Palucca-Schule
Gera	Ernst Laube
Lüneburg	Geheimrat Snell
Magdeburg	Stabsarzt Lieschke
Meuselwitz	Kurt Herrmann
Mülheim-Ruhr	Heide Woog
Pforzheim	Ingeborg Roon
Ratibor	Elinor Warsitz
Potsdam	Olga Fricke
Weimar	Alice Magdeburg
Kassel	Elisabeth Klemm
Karlsruhe	Josef Harald Fürstenau
Soest (Westfalen)	Motta Nolling
Kairo	Dr Peters

Additional local groups listed in 'Schrifttanz' May 1929:

Mannheim	Harry Pierenkämper
Celle i. Ha.	Gusti Bornhöft
Erfurt	Werner Fröbisch
Bonn a. Rh.	Käte Jungmann

22 International Council of Kinetography Laban, 1959 and 1989

In 1959 the International Council of Kinetography Laban was started through the initiative of Lisa Ullmann. The people invited were individuals known to be leading the field in their own country. The back-up for each member varied from none for the Icelandic member to the large resources of the New York Dance Notation Bureau for Ann Hutchinson.

ICKL was necessary because the Nazi era and the war had divided the key developers. Knust had managed to work on quietly in Munich after the 1936 embargo on Laban work, and by 1959 was reestablished at the Folkwangschule in Essen, with more opportunities for using notation in the folk dance and ballet field than in any other. Ann Hutchinson was extremely active promoting notation primarily for dance theatre, where the varied styles of American modern dance influenced her way of analysing movement. Leeder was teaching in Switzerland, and had developed on from the analysis used in the Jooss/Leeder School, and Ullmann and Preston had remained with the original ways of writing and were concerned with creative dance and the need to use the notation in improvisation. Differences in method had inevitably crept in, some easily resolved but others requiring long discussion. There were contextual differences; the American 'selling' technique for the notation rubbed against the German careful academic approach, the Eastern bloc writers who were pressed for fine details for folk dance writing rubbed against the child-centred educational thinking of British notators. ICKL members began a long haul of reconciliation.

Founding membership of International Council of Kinetography Laban, 1959

ICKL was founded in 1959 'to further the system of movement notation originated by Rudolf Laban and to increase the world-wide understanding and acceptance of it'.

Founding membership:

Lisa Ullmann

Ann Hutchinson
Albrecht Knust
Sigurd Leeder

who were joined by:

Hungary	Emma Lugossy, Maria Szentpal
Poland	Roderyk Lange
Germany (DDR)	Ingeborg Baier
Iceland	Minerva Jondsdottir
United Kingdom	Diana Baddeley, Valerie Preston, Edna Geer
USA	Nadia Chilkovsky
Yugoslavia	Vera Maletic

ICKL membership in 1989
37 **Fellows** from USA, UK, Canada, W Germany, France, Iceland, Yugoslavia, Switzerland, Denmark, Hungary and Belgium.

52 **Members** from People's Republic of China, France, Netherlands, USA, Italy, UK, Poland, Switzerland, W Germany, Canada, Hong Kong, DDR and Hungary.

Many have established organisations or are working within institutions, such as the Juilliard School of Performing Arts, New York; Ohio State University; University of Hawaii; Centre for Dance Studies, Jersey; York University, Toronto; The Labanotation Institute, Surrey University, Guildford; Centre d'Écriture de Danse, Paris; The Language of Dance Centre, London.

The centre for Labanotation practice, reconstruction from scores, and teaching standards is the Dance Notation Bureau, 31 West 21st Street, New York, NY 10010, USA.

23 Laban Art of Movement Guild, 1958 and 1976

The Laban Art of Movement Guild started in 1946 as an organisation for the promotion of Laban's work, as an organ through which part-time training courses could be given, and as a meeting ground for supporters and practitioners of his work scattered in the UK.

Local Groups began to be formed almost immediately and the 1958 list of groups affiliated to the Guild illustrates their nature. Colleges for the training of teachers, such as Avery Hill Training College and Whitelands College, had a dance department which offered students not only teacher training but the opportunity for recreative and creative dance as an extra-curriular activity. Clubs, such as the Birmingham Contemporary Dance Club, the Ipswich Movement Group and the Manchester Dance Circle, offered regular meetings, similar to those of the movement choirs in Germany, in which training and the chance to participate in a dance work was given. Overseas groups began to appear, associated with a college of higher education or a university. They joined the LAMG because of general interest and because the Guild's magazine offered articles of a high standard (as well as anecdotal material).

The astounding increase in the number of affiliated groups, shown by the 1976 list, reflects the expansion of Laban's work in education which occurred in the 1960s and early 70s. The vast majority were institutions where the training and education of primary teachers, secondary PE teachers and secondary arts teachers took place. The expansion in overseas interest illustrates the influence of Laban's work in education abroad.

During the period immediately following 1976, the position rapidly altered in the UK. Instead of concentrating on the education of prospective teachers, the colleges diversified, offering 3-year degree courses in a variety of subjects with a fourth year in education studies for those people who wanted to make teaching their career. The switch from child-centred to subject-centred education was disastrous for Laban's work. In the first place he emphasised education of the person *through* dance, not education *in* dance, and in the second place very few colleges were in a position to offer, and to have accepted, a degree course in dance.

From the early 1970s pressure had already been put on dance

people with a Laban training to take training in American Modern
Dance, which became a staple ingredient of the new degree courses.
Many first-generation Laban pioneers were of retirement age, and
very few second-generation Laban trainees were sufficiently well-
educated or pioneering in spirit to withstand the onslaught. The
position in the UK by 1987 was that the LAM Guild might well
have collapsed altogether.

Laban Art of Movement Guild
Affiliated Groups, 1958
(compiled from LAMG News Sheet/Magazine)

Art of Movement Studio	Surrey
Avery Hill Training College	London
Birmingham Contemporary Dance Club	Birmingham
Bretton Hall College	Yorks
British Dance Theatre	Surrey
University of California	Berkeley, USA
Chelsea College of PE	Sussex
University of Colorado	USA
Ipswich Movement Group	Suffolk
Lady Mabel College of PE	Yorks
London Dance Group	London
Manchester Dance Circle	Manchester
Manchester Training College	Manchester
I.M. Marsh College of PE	Liverpool
Merseyside Dance Group	Liverpool
C.F. Mott Training College	Liverpool
Newcastle and Stafford Dance Group	Staffs
University of Western Australia	Nedlands, Australia
West Riding Movement Study Group	Yorks
Whitelands College	London
Worcestershire Dance Group	Worcs

Laban Art of Movement Guild
Affiliated Groups, 1976

Aberdeen College of Education	Aberdeen
Adelaide College of Advanced Education	Australia
University of Alberta	Canada

College of All Saints	London
Anstey College of PE	Warwicks
Avery Hill College of Education	London
Balls Park College	Herts
Bedford College of Education	Bedford
Bedford College of PE	Bedford
Berkshire College of Education	Berks
Bingley College of Education	Yorks
Birmingham Contemporary Dance Club	Birmingham
University of Birmingham	Birmingham
Bishop Lonsdale College of Education	Derby
Bishop Otter College of PE	W Sussex
Bognor Regis College of Education	W Sussex
Bradford College	Bradford
Bretton Hall College of Education	Yorks
Brighton College of Education	Brighton
Bristol Movement Association	Bristol
British Council	London
British Dance-Drama Theatre	Surrey
Brycbox Youth Arts Workshop	Surrey
University of California	Berkeley, USA
Cardiff Dance Circle	Cardiff
Chelsea College of PE	E Sussex
Christ's College	Liverpool
Claremont Teachers College	Claremont, Australia
Coloma College of Education	Kent
Coventry College of Education	Coventry
Craigie College of Education	Ayr
Crewe College of Education	Cheshire
Dalcroze Society	London
Darlington College of Education	Durham
Dartford College of PE	Kent
Didsbury College of Education	Manchester
Dormer High School	Warwick
Dudley College of Education	Worcs
Dunfermline College of PE	Edinburgh
University of Durban-Westville	Durban, S Africa
Maria Duschenes School	Sao Paulo, Brazil
Eastbourne Ballet Group	E Sussex

Eastbourne College of Education	E Sussex
Endsleigh College of Education	Hull
English Folk Dance & Song Society	London
Froebel Educational Institute	London
Furzedown College of Education	London
Glamorgan College of Education	Glamorgan
Glasgow Modern Dance Group	East Kilbride
Glenrothes Technical College	Glenrothes
Goldsmiths' College	London
Gwent Education Committee	Gwent
Gymnastik och Idrottschogskola	Stockholm, Sweden
Hereford College of Education	Hereford
Hertfordshire Teachers' Dance Group	Herts
Homewood Secondary School	Kent
Huddersfield Polytechnic	Huddersfield
ILEA College of PE	London
Jordanhill College of Education	Glasgow
Kennarahaskoli Islands	Reykjavik, Iceland
Keswick Hall College of Education	Norfolk
King Alfred's College	Hants
Laban Art of Movement Centre	Surrey
Lady Mabel College of PE	Yorks
Lady Spencer-Churchill College of Education	Oxford
City of Leeds & Carnegie College of Education	Leeds
University of Leeds	Leeds
Leicester College of Education	Leicester
Limerick National Institute for Higher Education	Limerick, Ireland
Liverpool Dance Workshop	Lancs
London Dance Theatre Group	London
University of London	London
Loughborough College of Education	Leics
McMaster University	Hamilton, Canada
McMillan College of Education	Yorks
Madeley College of Education	Cheshire
Manchester Dance Circle	Cheshire
Manchester College of Education	Manchester
University of Manchester	Manchester
Maria Grey College of Education	Middx

Marian Thomas School of Modern Dance	Fort Victoria, Rhodesia
I.M. Marsh College of PE	Liverpool
Mather College	Manchester
Matlock College of Education	Derbys
Middlesex Polytechnic	Herts
Mitchell College of Advanced Education	Bathurst, Australia
C.F. Mott College of Education	Liverpool
Neville's Cross College	Durham
Newcastle upon Tyne Polytechnic	Newcastle upon Tyne
Newland Park College of Education	Bucks
Newton Park College	Avon
Nonington College Dance Group	Kent
Norfolk Art of Movement Group	Norfolk
North Brisbane College of Advanced Education at Kedron Park	Kedron, Australia
University of North Carolina, Charlotte	Charlotte, USA
Northern Counties College	Newcastle upon Tyne
Northern Ireland Polytechnic	Co Antrim
Northumberland College of Education	Newcastle upon Tyne
Oxfordshire Dance Group	Oxon
Paddington School	London
Perpetuum Mobile	Kent
Physical Education Association of GB & NI	London
Portuguese Ministry of National Education	Lisbon, Portugal
Educacao e Movemento	Lourenco Marques, Mocambique
Polytechnic of North London	London
Portsmouth College of Education	Hants
Potchefstroom University	Potchefstroom, S Africa
Poulton le Fylde College of Education	Lancs
Queen's School for Girls	Cambs
University of Queensland	Brisbane, Australia
W. J. Rooney Library	W Perth, Australia

St John's College	York
College of St Mark & St John	Devon
St Martin's College of Education	Lancaster
St Mary's College	Gwynedd
St Mary's College	Glos
College of St Matthias	Bristol
St Paul's College of Education	Warwicks
Saffron Walden College	Essex
Sedgley Park College of Music	Manchester
Sheffield College of Education	Sheffield
Shenstone New College	Worcs
Sports Council	London
Sunderland Polytechnic	Durham
Swanley School	Kent
The Teachers' College	Bulawayo, Rhodesia
Trinity & All Saints College	Leeds
State College of Victoria	Kew, Australia
Welsh Folk Dance Society	Swansea
Western Australia Secondary Teachers' College	Nedlands, Australia
University of Western Australia	Nedlands, Australia
Westhill College of Education	Birmingham
West Midlands College of Education	Staffs
West Midlands Sports Council	Birmingham
Westminster College	Oxford
Weymount College of Education	Dorset
Whitelands College	London
Wingate Institute	Natanya, Israel
Worcester College of Education	Worcester
Yorkshire & Humberside Sports Council	Leeds
Yorkshire Movement Study Group	York

24 Some principal writings about Laban's work and influence

Since this book is an introductory one centred on Laban's life, the writings listed are those which resulted from direct contact with him, or those which reflect on his life. Later developments by individuals are not included.

Au, Susan, 'A man of movement: Rudolf Laban', *Dance Magazine* (June 1979), p. 102–105.

Aubel, Hermann & Marianne, *Der Künstlerische Tanz unserer Zeit (Artistic Dance of Our Time)* (K. R. Wiesche Verlag, Königstein/Taunus & Leipzig, 1930).

Auerbach, Lotte, 'My Memories of Laban', *LAMG Magazine* (No. 51, 1973).

Bach, Rudolf, 'Vom Wesen der Gruppenregie' ('The nature of group direction'), *Deutschen Tanzfestspiele 1934* (Carl Reissner Verlag, Dresden, 1934), pp. 50–59.

Bartenieff, Irmgard, with Lewis, Dori, *Body Movement: Coping with the Environment* (Gordon & Breach, New York, 1981).

Bereska, Dussia, 'Männlicher oder weiblicher Tanz?' ('Male or female dance?'), *Junge Menschen* (September 1923), pp. 197–198.
'Von der Tanzkunst' ('About the art of dance'), *Die Schönheit* (Heft 1, 1926), pp. 20–29.

Bergeest, Karl, 'Ein Stück des Wegs mit Rudolf von Laban/Bei Laban 1923 bis 1925 in Hamburg' ('Part of the way with Rudolf von Laban/with Laban in Hamburg 1923 to 1925'), *Das Tanzarchiv* (May 1973), pp. 361–363.

Bergengrün, Siegfried, 'Der Tanz erobert die Bühne' ('Dance conquers the stage'), *Der Tanz* (July 1930), pp. 2–4.

Berlin Staatstheater, Leaflet giving advance information for the season 1933/34.

Berliner Staatsoper, Open letter from General-Intendant of Prussian State Theatres (25 June 1931), urging that Laban's

contract as Choreographic Overseer 1 September 1930 to 31 August 1931 should be extended by 3 years (Laban Collection 213.01-.02).
200 Year Jubilee Book (M. Hesses Verlag, Berlin, 1942), 2 pages with pictures of Laban's *Dornröschen* of 1934.

Der Bewegungschor (15 July 1928), special issue for the Second Dancers' Congress in Essen.

Bie, Oscar, *Der Tanz (Dance)* (Julius Bard Verlag, Berlin, 1923).
'Der moderne Tanz' ('The modern dance'), *Schweizer Illustrierte Zeitung* (No. 7, 1925).
'Der Tanz' ('Dance'), *Jahrbuch* of Stadttheater, Bremen (Season 1926-27), pp. 93-96.
'Aus der Geschichte des Gesellschafts und Bühnentanzes' ('From the history of social and stage dance'), *Die Tat* (November 1927), pp. 609–610.
'Tanz und Musik in Berlin' ('Dance and music in Berlin'), *Stuttgarter neue Tagblatt* (24 February 1932). Deplores that Laban is doing nothing significant at the Staatsoper, Berlin.

Biedrzynski, Richard, 'Das städtische Ballett' ('The City Ballet'), *Deutsche Zeitung* (10 April 1927).

Blass, Ernst, 'Das Wesen der neuen Tanzkunst' ('The nature of the new art of dance'), *Die Neue Schaubühne* (September 1921) pp. 109–112.
Das Wesen der neuen Tanzkunst (The Nature of the New Art of Dance) (E. Lichtenstein, Weimar, 1921).

Blümner, Rudolf, 'Tanz und Tanz' ('Dance and dance'), *Der Sturm* (April 1926), p. 50.

Bodmer, Sylvia, 'Group Dancing', *Journal of Physical Education and School Hygiene* (November 1943), pp. 135–138.
'Rudolf Laban 1879–1958', *The New Era* (May 1959), p. 90.

Boehme, Fritz, *Der Tanz der Zukunft (The Dance of the Future)* (Delphin Verlag, München, 1926).
Tanzkunst (The Art of Dance) (C. Dünnhaupt Verlag, Dessau, 2nd edition, 1926).
'Vom Tänzer unserer Zeit' ('Dancers of our time'), *Die Tat* (November 1927), pp. 580–588.
'Anfänge der Tanznotation' ('The beginnings of dance notation'), *Der Scheinwerfer* (June 1928), pp. 4–6.

'Ein Kapitel aus der Geschichte der Choreographie' ('A chapter from the history of "Choreographie" '), *Schrifttanz* (July 1928), pp. 6–8.

'Choreologie und Tanzschrift' (' "Choreologie" and dance notation'), *Singchor und Tanz* (1928), pp. 155–156.

Entsiegelung der Geheimnisse: Zeichen der Seele zur Metaphysik der Bewegung (Unlocking the Secrets: Signs of the soul towards the metaphysics of movement) (Kinetischer Verlag, Berlin, 1928).

'Labans tänzerischer Nachwuchs' ('Laban's new generation of dancers'), *Schrifttanz* (December 1929), pp. 66–68.

'Podiumtanz und Theatertanz' ('Dance recitals and theatre dance'), *Singchor und Tanz* (15 June 1930), pp. 185–187.

'Vorstellung und Erlebnis im Tanz' ('Performance and experience in dance'), *Schrifttanz* (June 1930), pp. 37–39.

'Deutscher Tanz und Volkstanz' ('German dance and folk dance'), *Deutsche Tanzfestspiele 1934* (Carl Reissner Verlag, Dresden), pp. 37–43.

Boehn, Max von, *Der Tanz (Dance)* (Wegweiser Verlag, Berlin, 1925), pp. 1; 120–30.

Bojarzin, Otto, 'Reigentänze', *Der Vortrupp* (April 1914), pp. 249–252.

Brandenburg, Hans, *Der moderne Tanz (The Modern Dance)* (G. Müller, München, 2nd enlarged edition, 1917).

Das Theater und das neue Deutschland (The Theatre and the New Germany) (E. Diederichs, Jena, 1919).

'Uber Rudolf von Laban', *Die Tat* (December 1920), pp. 678–685.

Der moderne Tanz (The Modern Dance) (G. Müller, München, 3rd edition 1921), pp. 175–204.

'Die Tanzkunst in Deutschland' ('The art of dance in Germany'), *Hamburger Fremdenblatt* (10 January 1925), p. 19.

'Rudolf von Labans "Schwingende Gewalten" ', *Die Freude* (September 1925), pp. 392–397.

'Zur Einführung' ('As introduction'), *Die Tat* (November 1927), pp. 569–572.

'Tanz und Theater' ('Dance and theatre'), *Die Tat* (November 1927), pp. 605–609.

'Schrifttanz und Bühne' ('Dance literacy and theatre'), *Schrifttanz* (July 1928), pp. 9–10.

'Solotanz und Gruppentanz' ('Solo dance and group dance'), *Singchor und Tanz* (Heft 12, 1928), pp. 159–160.

'Rudolf von Laban', *Deutsche Tonkünstler-Zeitung* (5 December 1929), pp. 729–730.

'Rudolf von Laban zu seinem 50. Geburtstage' ('Laban—on the occasion of his 50th birthday'), *Blätter des Stadttheater Stettin* (December 1929).

'Erinnerungen an Labans Anfänge' ('Memories of Laban's begin- nings'), *Schrifttanz* (December 1929), pp. 70–71.

'Laban als Stilreformer' ('Laban as a reformer of style'), *Singchor und Tanz* (Heft 24, 1929), pp. 297–298.

'Von deutscher Tanzkunst' ('About the German art of dance'), *Deutsche Tanzfestpiele 1934* (Carl Reissner Verlag, Dresden).

'Der Tanz und unsere Zeit' ('Dance and our time'), *Tanz und Reigen* (ed. G. Ignaz, Bühnenvolksbundverlag, Berlin, 1927), pp. 8–11.

Brandt, Rosemary, 'An Application of Rudolf Laban's Principles of Human Movement to the Generating Principles of Classical Ballet' (MA Thesis, Laban Centre, London, 1987).

Brandt-Knack, Olga, 'Mein Weg zu Rudolf von Laban' ('My road to Rudolf von Laban'), *Singchor und Tanz* (Heft 24, 1929), p. 303.

Braur, Fritz, 'Einblick in die Deutsche Tanzkultur' ('A view of German dance culture'), *Der Tanz* (Heft 14, 1929).

British Journal of Physical Education (July 1977), special feature 'Dance in Education', pp. 109–116.

Bruce, Violet, *Dance and Dance Drama in Education* (Pergamon Press, Oxford, 1965).

Büro des internationalen Tanzwettgewerbe gelegentlich der XI. Olympiade, Internal memos re staffing (June 1936); auditors' report (22 August 1936); further memos re staffing (Laban Collection 209.28-.45).

Burger, August, 'Die Fachschaft Tanz', *Deutsche Tanzzeitschrift* (April 1936), pp. 7–8.

Burghardt, Wilm, 'Rudolf von Laban', *Die Schönheit* (Heft 1, 1926), pp. 4–19.
'Der männliche Tänzer' ('The male dancer'), *Die Schönheit* (Heft 2, 1926), pp. 69–83.

Carroll, J. and Lofthouse, P., *Creative Dance for Boys* (Macdonald & Evans, London, 1969).

Coton, A.V., 'The Sigurd Leeder School of Dance', *Movement* (Vol. 1, No. 2, Winter 1948), pp. 23-26; 32.
The New Ballet: Kurt Jooss and his work (Dennis Dobson, London, 1946).

Curl, Gordon, 'A Critical Study of Rudolf von Laban's Theory and Practice of Movement' (MEd Thesis, Leicester University, 1967).

Crabbe, M. T., 'Laban's Influence upon Physical Education in England', *The New Era* (May 1959), pp. 103-104.

Degeners Wer ist's (Degener's Who's Who) (Hermann Degener, Berlin, 10th edition, 1935), p. 920, entry for Rudolf von Laban.

Deutsche Allgemeine Zeitung (Berlin, 2 July 1934), review of farewell *matinée* of Laban's work presented by Kraft durch Freude at Staatsoper, Berlin, in the presence of Adolf Hitler.

Deutscher Tänzerbund & Deutsche Tanzgemeinschaft, 'Plans for Dance in Higher Education', *Singchor und Tanz* (15 June 1930), pp. 198-199.

Diem, Liselott, 'Ein Gespräch mit Rudolf von Laban' ('A conversation with Rudolf von Laban'), *Leibeserziehung* (1 January 1959), p. 21. The conversation took place in Manchester in 1949.

Dunn, Margaret, 'Movement as an Aid to the Understanding and Development of Personality', Hull University, Conference Report *Movement, Dance and Drama* (March 1970).

Ellis, C. D., 'The Use of Laban/Lawrence Effort Assessments in Promoting Good Industrial Relations', *LAMG News Sheet* (No. 10, March 1953), pp. 1-26.

Emmel, Felix, 'Neue Sachlichkeit im Tanz' ('New functionalism in dance'), *Tanzgemeinschaft* (No. 3, 1930), pp. 4-5.

Englische Rundschau (22 July 1951), feature 'Rudolf Laban und seine Tanznoten' ('Rudolf Laban and his dance notation'). This is a translation, slightly shortened, of the 'Profile' in *The Observer* of the same date.

Feist, Herta, 'Laban unserer Wegbereiter' ('Laban, our forerunner'), Lecture given in Hannover, 6 November 1954 (Laban Archives).

Feist-Lichterfeld, Hertha, 'Ein Stück des Wegs mit Laban' ('A part of the way with Laban'), *Das Tanzarchiv* (May 1976), pp. 164–170.

Fischer, Hans W., 'Zukunft des Tanzes' ('The future of dance'), *Junge Menschen* (September 1923), pp. 194–195.
'Der moderne Tanz und das Theater' ('Modern dance and the theatre'), *Rheinisch-Westfälische Zeitung* (2 July 1928).

Flanagan, Hallie, 'Kurt Jooss at Dartington Hall', *Theatre Arts Monthly* (May 1934), pp. 337–9.

Foster, John, *The Influence of Rudolph Laban* (Lepus Books, London, 1977).

Gena, Gerda, 'Das Tannhäuser-Bacchanal in den Bayreuther Festspielen' ('The "Bacchanale" in *Tannhäuser* at the Bayreuth festival'), *Der Tanz* (October 1930), pp. 18–19.

Gentges, Ignaz (ed), *Tanz und Reigen* (Bühnenvolksbundverlag, Berlin, 1927), pp. 69-80. Articles by Wigman and Laban.

Gertz, Jenny, 'Tanz und Kind' ('Dance and the child'), *Die Schönheit* (Heft 2, 1926), pp. 49–61.
'Bewegungschor und Proletariat' ('Movement choir and proletariat'), *Am Wege* (March 1930), pp. 43–44.

Gleisner, Martin, Report on Second Dancers' Congress, Essen 1928, *Die Tat* (September 1928), pp. 473–475.
Tanz für Alle: Von der Gymnastik zum Gemeinschaftstanz (Dance for All: From gymnastics to communal dance) (Hesse & Becker, Leipzig, 1928).
'Laban als Schöpfer des Laientanzes' ('Laban as the creator of amateur dance'), *Der Tanz* (December 1929), pp. 5–6.
'Laban als Wegbahner des Tanzes für die Allgemeinheit' ('Laban as a pioneer for making dance accessible to everybody'), *Singchor und Tanz* (15 December 1929), p. 301.
'Kind und Tanz' ('The child and dancing'), *Die Jugendbühne* (February 1931), pp. 7–9.
'Festspiel *Rotes Lied*', *Schrifttanz* (October 1931), p. 37.
Letter to Ilse Loesch of 7 July 1977 (Laban Collection 207.39-

.43). Contains Gleisner's reminiscences from 1915 to 1937 and other historical information.

Godlewski, Willy, 'Ballett contra Ausdruckstanz' ('Ballet versus modern dance'), *Singchor und Tanz* (15 April 1931), p. 105.

Green, Martin, *Mountain of Truth* (Tufts University Press, Hanover and London, 1986).

Gulbenkian Foundation, Calouste, *Dance Education and Training in Great Britain* (1980) p. 192.

Güldenstein, Gustav, 'Grundlagen zu einer Tanzkultur' ('Bases for a dance culture'), *Schrifttanz* (June 1930), pp. 23–24.

Günther, Dorothee, 'Warum Tanzpädagogik?' ('Why educational theory of the dance?'), *Schrifttanz* (November 1930), pp. 45–47.

Günther, Johannes, 'Tanz und Schauspiel' ('Dance and Drama'), *Deutsche Tanzfestspiele 1934* (Carl Reissner Verlag, Dresden), pp. 43–59.

Gürster, Eugen, 'Das tänzerische Element in der szenischen Darstellung' ('The dance element in drama'), *Die neue Schaubühne* (August 1920), pp. 201–205.

Hall, Fernau, 'An Interview with Jooss', *Dancing Times* (November 1945), pp. 55–7.

Hamburger Tanzschreibstube, *Die Kinetogramm-Veröffentlichungen der Hamburger Tanzschreibstube (The kinetogram publications of the Hamburg notation centre)* (undated).

Herrmann, Marion, 'Der Tanz—eine Aufgabe' ('Dance—a task'), *Berliner Tageblatt* (18 October 1935).

Hilker, Franz, 'Was uns Not tut' ('What causes us distress'), *Künstlerischehe Körperschulung*, Pallat, L. and Hilker, F. (eds) (Ferdinand Hirt, Breslau, 1925), pp. 9–13.

Hodgson, John, *Improvisation* (Methuen, London, 1974).
    (Ed), *Uses of Drama* (Methuen, London, 1972).

Hüser, Fritz, 'Aufwärts! Die Bedeutung des Bewegungschores' ('Upwards! The meaning of the movement choir'), *Westfälische Allgemeine Volkszeitung* (28 August 1928).

Jacob, Walter, 'Zu den Bewegungschören Rudolf von Labans'

('About Rudolf von Laban's movement choirs'), *Die Schönheit* (Heft 1, 1926) pp. 30–41.

Jooss, Kurt, 'Tanzkunst' ('The art of dance'), *Der Scheinwerfer* (March 1928), p. 23.
'Rudolf von Laban und das Ballett' ('Rudolf von Laban and the ballet'), *Singchor und Tanz* (Heft 24, 1929), pp. 296–297.

Jordan, Diana, *The Dance as Education* (Oxford University Press, London, 1938).

Junk, Victor, *Handbuch des Tanzes (Handbook for dance)* (G. Olms Verlag, 1977, first published 1929).

Kammer-Tanzbühne Laban, Press reviews 1925–1926 (reviews from 14 cities; list of 46 works in repertoire) (Laban Collection 164.17-.24).

Klingenbeck, Fritz, 'Der tanzende Festzug' ('The dancing procession'), *Schrifttanz* (May 1929), pp. 27–28.
'Was aufschreiben und was nicht?' ('What should one write down and what not?'), *Schrifttanz* (November 1930), pp. 48–49.

Knust, Albrecht, 'Sinn und Weg des neuen Laientanzes' ('Purpose and meaning of the new amateur dance'), in leaflet from Laban Tanzbühne (after 1923). (Laban Collection 123.16).
'Laban als Erzieher' ('Laban as educator'), *Singchor und Tanz* (15 December 1929).
'Hamburg im Tanz' ('Hamburg dancing'), *Der Zeitungshandler* (24 June 1933), pp. 1–7.
'Die Entwicklung der chorischen Idee in Hamburg' ('The development of the movement choir idea in Hamburg'). Typescript of a talk given in Hamburg in March 1934. (Laban Collection 026.41-.46).
'The Development of the Laban Kinetography (Part I)', *Movement* (Summer 1948), pp. 28–29.
'The Development of the Laban Kinetography (Part II)', *Movement* (Winter 1948), pp. 27–28.
'The Validity of Laban's Art of Movement and Notation', *The New Era* (May 1959), p. 105.

Koch, Hermann, 'Unsere Lebensgestaltung und Laban' ('Our lifestyle and Laban'), *Am Wege* (January 1930), pp. 7–9.

Koegler, Horst, 'In the Shadow of the Swastika: Dance in

Germany 1929-1936', *Dance Perspectives* 57 (Spring 1974).

Lämmel, Rudolf, *Der moderne Tanz* (Modern dance), (Oestergaard Verlag, Berlin, 1927).
'Tanz und Erziehung' ('Dance and education'), *Singchor und Tanz* (Heft 12, 1928), pp. 156–158.

Lamb, Warren, 'Laban's Contribution to Effectiveness in Work', *The New Era* (May 1959), pp. 106–110.
Posture and Gesture (Duckworth, London, 1965).

Lewitan, J., 'Der Kampf um den Tanz' ('The struggle for dance'), a report on a lecture of the same title given by Laban, *Der Tanz* (May 1929), pp. 2–3.
'Laban, der Tanz-Tribun', *Der Tanz* (December 1929), pp. 6–7.
'Laban an der Spitze des Staatsopernballetts!' ('Laban has become the head of the State Opera ballet!'), *Der Tanz* (Heft 5, 1930), p. 2.
'Sündenbock Laban/Zur Kündigung der Solisten der Staatsoper' ('Laban the scapegoat/On the dismissal of the soloists of the State Opera'), *Der Tanz* (May 1931), p. 2.

Lieschke, Marie Luise, 'Von der deutsche Tanzbühne' ('About the "Deutsche Tanzbühne" '), *Singchor und Tanz* (1 August 1935), pp. 107–108.

Litterscheid, Richard, 'Essen feiert Laban's 50. Geburtstag' ('Essen celebrates Laban's 50th birthday'), *Der Tanz* (February 1930), pp. 11–12.

Loesch, Ilse, 'Kinder im neuen Geist' ('Children in a new spirit'), *Der Tanz* (September 1932), pp. 4–5.

Loeszer, Gert Ruth, Publicity leaflet (1925) for duet programmes by Loeszer and Laban, some based on Wagner operas, some without music. Contains extracts from numerous press notices, with names of cities and theatres played in. (Laban Collection 204.45-.47).

Maack, Rudolf, *Tanz in Hamburg* (1975), pp. 5–12.
'Labans Hamburger Jahre (1922-1925)' ('Laban's Hamburg years (1922–1925)'), *Die Tanzarchivreihe* (No. 19/20 *Laban*, 1979), pp. 11–15.

Macdonald & Evans, Advertisement of Laban's books in English, *Movement* (Summer 1948), p. iii.

Main Currents in Modern Thought (Vol. 31, No. 1, September-October 1974), issue devoted to Laban.

Maletic, Vera, *Body—Space—Expression* (Mouton de Gruyter, Berlin, 1987).

Markard, Anna and Markard, Hermann, *Jooss Exhibition* catalogue (Folkwang Museum, Essen, 1985).

Meier, Walli, 'The Influence of Rudolf Laban's Work on the Development of the Keep Fit Association of England and Wales', *LAMG Magazine* (No. 36, May 1966), pp. 30–3.

Meredith-Jones, Betty, 'Rudolf Laban as a Teacher', *The New Era* (May 1959), pp. 115–116.

Michel, Artur, 'Der absolute Tanz' ('Pure dance'), *Vossische Zeitung* (Berlin) (5 February 1924).

Milloss, Aurel von, 'Professor Labans Werk' ('Prof Laban's work'), *Neue Zeit* (1927).

Milloss, Aurelio M., 'Laban: l'apertura di una nuove era nella storia della danza' ('Laban: the opening of a new era in the history of dance'), Di Gacomo (ed) *Tanztheater—della danza espressionista a Pina Bausch* (Roma, 1982).

Ministry of Education, *Moving and Growing* (HM Stationery Office, London, 1953).

Ministry of Propaganda (Germany), Laban's Contract (20 April 1936) as Director of Meisterwerkstätten für Tanz e.V., 1 May 1936 to 31 March 1937, with ms note of Laban's agreement to resign as from 1 November 1936. (Laban Collection 212.56-.58).

Mönckeberg-Kollmar, Vilma, 'Laban und das "Tänzerische Theater" ' ('Laban and theatre with dance'), *Tanzarchivreihe* (No. 19/20 *Laban*, 1979), pp. 19–23.

Monte Verità—Berg der Wahrheit (Monte Verità—Mountain of Truth), catalogue of exhibition at Ascona (c. 1980).

Morrison, Ruth, *Educational Gymnastics* (Private publication, Liverpool, 1956).

Müller, Grete, 'Zwei Pioniere des Ausdruckstanzes in Europa/ Sigurd Leeder, Rudolf von Laban' ('Two pioneers of expressionist dance in Europe/Sigurd Leeder, Rudolf von Laban'), in the periodical of the Swiss Association for Dancers and Gymnasts, No. 2, 1983.

Müller-Rau, Elli, 'Laientanz als Kulturfaktor' ('Amateur dance as a cultural factor'), *Kulturwille* (No. 5, 1928).

Neher, Caspar, *Wagner-Régeny, Begegnungen* (1968), pp. 50–59.

Neue Zeitung (4 November 1953), 'Vom Fest zur Arbeit' ('From festival to work'), report of an interview with Laban at Addlestone.

The New Era/in Home and School (May 1959), special issue on Rudolf Laban.

Niedecken-Gebhard, Hanns, 'Tanz und Bühne' ('Dance and stage'), *Die Tat* (November 1927), pp. 618-621.

North, Marion, 'What Laban did for People', *The New Era* (May 1959), pp. 110–113.
A Simple Guide to Movement Teaching (Private publication, London, 1959).
Composing Movement Sequences (Private publication, London, 1961).
'Movement—A New Academic Field?', *Bulletin* (University of London Institute of Education, Summer Term 1968), pp. 7–13.
An Introduction to Movement Study and Teaching (Macdonald & Evans, London, 1971).
Personality Assessment Through Movement (Macdonald & Evans, London, 1972, reissued by Northcote House, Plymouth, 1990).

The Observer (22 July 1951), feature 'Profile' of Rudolf Laban.

Peters, Kurt, 'An Rudolph von Laban' ('To Rudolph von Laban'), *Tanz Prisma* (December 1950), pp. 3; 20.
'Brennpunkt Laban' ('Flashpoint Laban'), *Tanzarchivreihe* (No. 19/20 Laban, 1979), pp. 30–33.

Peters-Rohse, Gisela, 'Rudolf von Labans einhundertster Geburtstag im internationalen Jahr des Kindes' ('Rudolf von Laban's hundredth birthday in the International Year of the Child'), *Das Tanzarchiv* (March 1979), pp. 118–120.

Preston-Dunlop, Valerie, *A Handbook for Modern Educational*

Dance (Macdonald & Evans, London, 1963).

Readers in Kinetography Laban (Macdonald & Evans, London, 1966–67).

Practical Kinetography Laban (Macdonald & Evans, London, 1969.)

'Towards an understanding of Rudolf Laban's cultural environment', *Working Papers in Dance Studies* (Vol. 1, 1987).

'Towards an Understanding of Rudolf Laban and the Third Reich', *Dance Theatre Journal* (July 1988).

and Purkis, Charlotte, 'Rudolf Laban—the Making of Modern Dance: The Seminal Years in Munich 1910-14', *Dance Theatre Journal* (Winter 1989).

Prinz, Harry, 'Laban's Festzug der Gewerbe in Wien' ('Laban's procession of the guilds in Vienna'), *Der Tanz* (July 1929), pp. 8–10.

Randall, M., *Basic Movement* (G. Bell & Son, London, 1961).

Redfern, Betty, *Introducing Laban Art of Movement* (Macdonald & Evans, London, 1965).

Reichsbund für Gemeinschaftstanz, *Wir tanzen* (Berlin, 1936), gives details of *Vom Tauwind und der neuen Freude*, choreog. Laban.

Reimann Musik-Lexikon (Schott, Mainz, 12th edition, 1961), Vol: 'Personente L–Z', p. 1, entry for Rudolf von Laban.

Robertson, Seonaid: 'Talking with Laban', *The New Era* (May 1959), pp. 113–115.

Russell, Joan, *Modern Dance in Education* (Macdonald & Evans, London, 1958).

Creative Dance in the Primary School (Macdonald & Evans, London, 1965, reissued by Northcote House, Plymouth, 1987).

Creative Dance in the Secondary School (Macdonald & Evans, London, 1969).

Rutherston, Jeanette, 'The Central European Dance in England', *Dancing Times* (December 1934), pp. 313–6.

Schikowski, John, *Der neue Tanz (The new dance)* (Volksbühnenverlag, Berlin, 1927), chapters on Laban and Wigman, pp. 37–51.

Schlee, Alfred, 'Wo steht Laban?' ('Where is Laban now?'), *Der Tanz* (December 1929), pp. 4–5.
'An der Wende des neuen Tanzes' ('At the turning point of new dance'), *Schrifttanz* (April 1930), pp. 1–2.

Schmidts, Margarethe, 'Tänzerische Gymnastik nach Rudolf v. Laban' ('Dance-like gymnastics according to Rudolf v. Laban'), Pallat, Ludwig and Hilker, Franz, *Künstlerische Körperschulung* (Ferdinand Hirt, Breslau, 1925), pp. 55–57.

Schrifttanz (December 1929), pp. 65–82, Laban's 50th birthday.

Schuftan, Werner, *Handbuch des Tanzes (Handbook for dance)* (Verlag Deutscher Chorsängerverband und Tänzerbund e.V., Mannheim, undated).
'Labans Bewegungsschrift' ('Laban's notation of movement'), *Singchor und Tanz* (Heft 24, 1929), p. 302.

Scope: Magazine for Industry (October 1954) 'Man of the Month (153) Rudolf Laban', pp. 60–72; 86, relates to Laban-Lawrence Test.

Singchor und Tanz (Heft 12, 1928), 'Kongressnummer'.
(15 December 1929), 'Festnummer Laban', for his 50th birthday.
(15 June 1930), 'Kongressnummer'.

Skoronel, Vera & Laban, Rudolf von, 'Zwei Äusserungen zum II. Deutschen Tänzerkongress' ('Two comments on the 2nd German Dancers' Congress'), *West-Woche* (June 1928), pp. 10–11.
'Laban', *Singchor und Tanz* (Heft 24, 1929), pp. 299–300.

Snell, Gertrud, 'Tanzwissenschaft' ('Dance as an academic discipline'), *Die Schönheit* (Heft 2, 1926), pp. 62–68.
'Grundlagen einer allgemeinen Tanzlehre' ('Fundamentals of a general theory of dance'), *Schrifttanz* (January 1929), pp. 8–11.
'Grundlagen einer allgemeinen Tanzlehre—II. Choreologie' ('Fundamentals of a general theory of dance—II, Choreology'), *Schrifttanz* (May 1929), pp. 21–24.
'Grundlagen einer allgemeinen Tanzlehre—III, Eukinetik' ('Fundamentals of a general theory of dance—III, Eukinetics'), *Schrifttanz* (August 1929).

Snell-Friedburg, Gertrud, 'Die Geburt des Ikosaeders und der

Kinetographie' ('The birth of the icosahedron and of Kinetography'), *Tanzarchivreihe* (No. 19/20 *Laban*, 1979), pp. 15–19.

Stadler, Edmund, 'Rudolf von Laban', Szeeman, Harald (ed) *Der Hang zum Gesamtkunstwerk (The tendency to synthesis in the arts)* (Catalogue of an exhibition: Zurich, Dusseldorf, Vienna, 1983), pp. 339–342.

Stefan, Paul (ed), *Tanz in dieser Zeit (Dance in our time)* (Universal-Edition, Vienna, undated). Articles by Laban, Wigman, Schlemmer, item on Laban's movement choirs.

Stephenson, Geraldine, 'Laban's influence on Dramatic Movement', *The New Era* (May 1959), pp. 98–102.

Suhr, Werner, 'Zu Rudolf von Labans 70. Geburtstag' ('On Rudolf von Laban's 70th birthday'), *Die Neue Zeitung* (15 December 1949).
Die Tat (November 1927), whole issue devoted to dance, following the Dancers' Congress at Magdeburg.

Thornton, Sam, *A Movement Perspective of Rudolf Laban* (Macdonald & Evans, London, 1971).

Trevelyan, John, 'Movement in Education (2)', *Movement* (Winter 1948).

Ullmann, Lisa, 'The Value I See in Laban's Ideas', *The New Era* (May 1959), pp. 94–98.
'Rudolf von Laban in England 1938–1958', *Tanzarchivreihe* (No. 19/20 *Laban*, 1979), pp. 26–28.

Walcher, Edith, ' "Musiker und Tänzer" und die Tanzschrift Rudolf von Labans' (' "Musicians and dancers" and Rudolf von Laban's dance notation'), *Singchor und Tanz* (1931), p. 87.

Warner, Mary Jane, *Labanotation Scores: An International Bibliography* (New York, 1984).

Wigman, Mary, 'Aus "Rudolf von Labans Lehre vom Tanz" ' ('From "Rudolf von Laban's theory of dance" '), *Die neue Schaubühne* (February 1921), pp. 30–35.
'Rudolf von Labans Lehre vom Tanz' ('Rudolf von Laban's theory of dance'), *Die neue Schaubühne* (September 1921), pp. 99–106.

'Rudolf von Laban zum Geburtstag' ("To Rudolf von Laban on his birthday'), *Schrifttanz* (December 1929), pp. 65–66.

'Rudolf von Laban', *Singchor und Tanz* (Heft 24, 1929), p. 295.

(ed and trans Sorell, Walter) *The Mary Wigman Book* (Wesleyan University Press, Middletown, Conn., 1975).

Wiles, John & Garrard, Alan, *Leap to Life* (Chatto & Windus, London, 1957).

Winearls, Jane, *Modern Dance: The Jooss-Leeder Method* (A & C Black, London, 1958).

Wulff, Käthe, 'Aus alten Briefen' ('From old letters'), *Schrifttanz* (December 1929), p. 72.

2nd Dancers' Congress in Essen (21–26 June 1928), *Programme* (Laban Collection 123.29-.30).

'Die Entschliessungen des Essener Tänzerkongresses' ('The decisions of the Essen Dancers' Congress'), unknown newspaper (1928) (Laban Collection 179.06).

3rd Dancers' Congress in Munich (1930)—Lectures given during the Congress by: R. Schulz-Dornburg, F. Emmel, H. Brandenburg, R. von Laban, F. Muckermann, M. Gleisner, F. Boehme, *Der Tanz* (Heft 8, 1930), pp. 2–10.

25 Laban, the graphic artist

The only formal professional training Laban ever had was in art. In Bratislava (then known as Poszony, in Hungary) while in his late teens he had served as apprentice to a local painter, who soon began to command Laban's respect.

From quite an early age Laban had found pleasure in sketching and painting. In these artistic endeavours, as in no other, the family admired, praised and encouraged him. It was something of a suprise, then, and his first taste of artistic discipline, when he showed his master painter these early efforts and found how keenly they could be criticised by the professional.

Laban's sister, Renée, reported how those years of apprenticeship taught him not just about fine art in particular but about art and artists in general. He learnt not only about brushwork and colour, but also about form and line, perspective and proportion. It was this master craftsman who first opened his eyes to the golden mean and geometric shape. Above all, he learnt from him how to transform looking and seeing into observing and analysing, all based upon a philosophy grounded in commitment, and an approach which saw work not as separated from, but related to and part of life itself.

Recent research has shown that for a while in Munich in 1900 he studied with the great art and crafts teacher Herman Obrist. Then, in Paris until 1907, he studied anatomy and architecture, as well as researching forms of dance notation. While in Paris, and later back in Munich, he earned a kind of meagre existence from his graphic work, although it always seemed that this was itself only a further means of developing skills which he would later use in a related field. From around 1912 he found himself totally immersed in the world of movement and dance.

For the rest of his days he was never very far from paper and pencil. He would make notes and scribble sketches at all times. He looked at figures or shapes, at reality or fantasy, he looked seriously or comically, and he recorded impressions and ideas on all kinds and qualities of paper.

The twelve illustrations of his graphic artistry reproduced here come from originals which have not previously been published and each shows a different aspect of his graphic work. Taken together, they also reveal a breadth which has not been apparent until now.

All the drawings are from John Hodgson's private Laban Collection, based on the archives preserved by Frau Marie Luise Lieschke.

1. Mythological (pencil sketch): captures something of his youthful fantasy and interest in landscape. The world around takes on supernatural forms overshadowing the individual beneath, a common theme in his imagination.

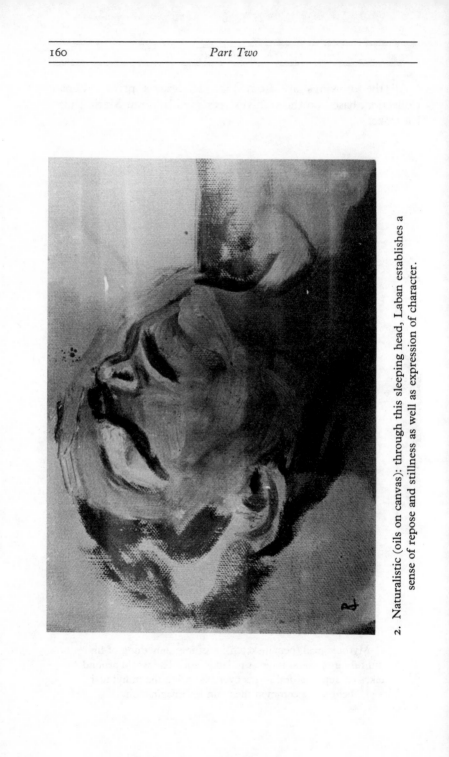

2. Naturalistic (oils on canvas): through this sleeping head, Laban establishes a sense of repose and stillness as well as expression of character.

3. Anatomical (ink drawing): Laban studied human muscle, sinew and bone structure, and began to put together 'a notebook of anatomical sketches', many in colour, expressing a detailed observation and understanding.

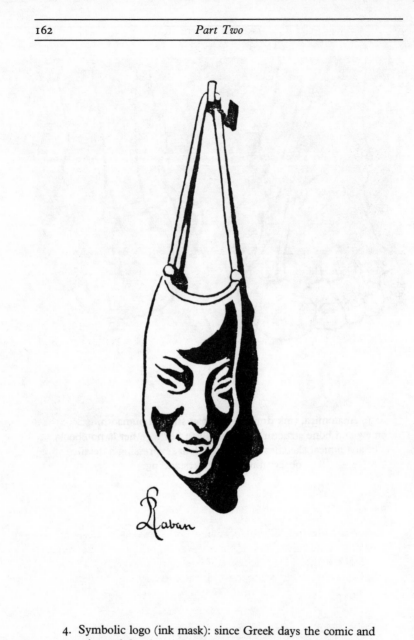

4. Symbolic logo (ink mask): since Greek days the comic and
tragic mask has been a common theatrical symbol, but here
Laban takes a fresh approach through this smiling face and
elongated shadow—one mask, two faces! This was the kind of
logo he offered commercially.

...eat many of Laban's figures
...rms. He saw three as an
...him to portray a range of
...of harmony and conflict.
...st the fixed lines.

5. Free flow (ink sketch): economically expressed in curves of
body and movement, this captures the spirit of Ascona—the nude
dancing, the circle, the sense of open air, of cooperation, of
flexibility, of sheer innocent pleasure in dancing together.

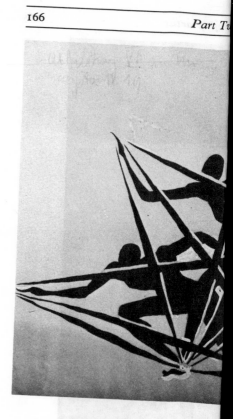

8. Geometric (brush and paint): a gr
   move in and around geometric fo
   effective dramatic number enabling
   level and effort as well as contrasts
   Moving curves work again

6. Costumed character (crayon drawing, black costume
red-faced mask): in the early days Laban frequently desig
costumes for his dances. His performers were fortunate to
able to wear costumes that were devised by the choreogra
himself who had not only a lively imagination, a vivid sen
shape and character, but also knew that these costumes we
dancers to dance in.

5. Free flow (ink sketch): economically expressed in curves of body and movement, this captures the spirit of Ascona—the nude dancing, the circle, the sense of open air, of cooperation, of flexibility, of sheer innocent pleasure in dancing together.

6. Costumed character (crayon drawing, black costume, red-faced mask): in the early days Laban frequently designed costumes for his dances. His performers were fortunate to be able to wear costumes that were devised by the choreographer himself who had not only a lively imagination, a vivid sense of shape and character, but also knew that these costumes were for dancers to dance in.

7. Pastiche (brush, pen and ink): Laban clearly enjoyed the *art nouveau* and the work of artists like Beardsley. He was able to capture his style yet, in his own way, balance the sense of impact, extravagance and movement with a touch of humour. Drawings like this were offered commercially to such magazines as *Jugend*.

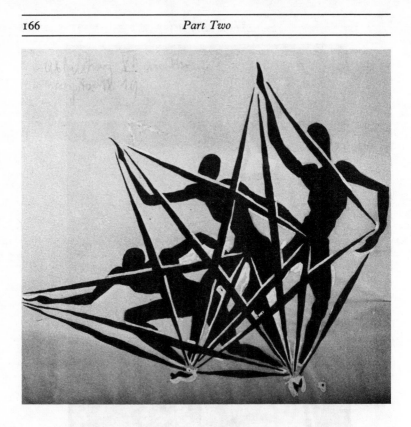

8. Geometric (brush and paint): a great many of Laban's figures move in and around geometric forms. He saw three as an effective dramatic number enabling him to portray a range of level and effort as well as contrasts of harmony and conflict. Moving curves work against the fixed lines.

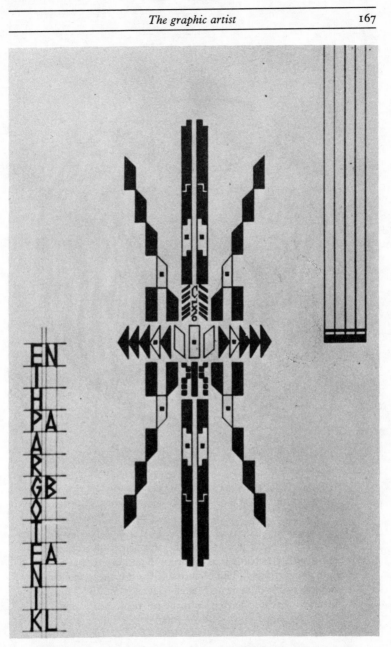

9. Mathematical abstract (pen and ink): using notation symbols
and his own name, Laban created a design which summarised a
great many aspects of his kinetography and emphasised its
comparability both with verbal and musical writing. He conveyed
a sense of movement while using straight lines throughout.

10. Lyrical sensual (pen and brush): this cameo-like drawing
brought together Laban's interest in myth and mystery as well as
strength and harmony. The picture itself is the circle, enclosing
the sensitive union of male and female, legend and life. This kind
of drawing would have been made for book illustration.

11. Grotesque comic (ink and brush): down to earth (or below it!), cutting the devil's toenails proves more of a problem than expected. Disproportion is portrayed with flowing curves and contrasting expressions. The unanticipated movement, the overextended limb, causes the eyeballs to bulge and the jaw to drop! This was the kind of drawing he made for friends.

12. Architectural sculpture (moulded clay): Laban sketched,
drew and designed a number of theatres and spaces for
movement work, but this model in clay combined many of his
ideas, especially that of dance as a three-dimensional art which
should be witnessed 'in the round'. In his day (and to a large
extent still) dance was presented to the front; a sculptured form
should be experienced in a sculptured space.

Index to Part One